BOMBER BROWN

The Tony Brown Story

Tony Brown, John Homer & Glenn Willmore

Perspective Publishing

First published in Great Britain in 1998 by
PERSPECTIVE PUBLISHING
54 Newhall Street
West Bromwich
West Midlands B70 7DJ

ISBN 0 9534626 0 9

Book and cover design by Glenn Willmore

Printed and bound in Great Britain by Redwood Books, Trowbridge

FOREWORD

Of all the pros I've had the pleasure of working with, Tony Brown stands among the highest. He won just a few internationals caps, he wasn't one of the 'glamour players' — but I cannot imagine a more highly valued team-mate. When I went to West Bromwich as player-manager, Tony was one of my great assets, and they included the young Bryan Robson, another great pro.

Tony was big-hearted and wonderfully talented in a brilliantly uncomplicated way. He was quick. He scored goals. He always knew what was happening around him. It was appropriate that when the Albion returned to the top flight with a win at Oldham, Tony should score the goal — the fruit of typical application and sure instinct around the goal. As a manager you wanted to give Tony the world. You wanted to get him the best terms, the best conditions — you always wanted to tell the board, 'Do you realise that his kind of player is pure gold?'.

One of the frustrations of management is that in this respect you cannot always get the right result. But in the end, Tony made his own reward — the respect of everyone who knew him and, most of all, played with him.

John Giles

INTRODUCTION

With football writing undergoing something of a boom at the moment, there have been plenty of books published recently about some of the well-known stars of today. When putting together this book, we felt it was time to record the career of a true professional who would, were he playing today, command a transfer fee in excess of £15m, and be earning, literally, in the millions.

Tony Brown's career was spread across the Sixties, Seventies and the early Eighties, when it was unfashionable to flit from club to club for monetary gain; when fidelity to one club was respected and admired and agents were an unnecessary evil.

In the dark days of Don Howe's spell at the Albion, Tony was virtually the only reason for coming to watch the side — if he failed to score, then, usually, so did the rest of the team. Later, under Giles, Allen and Atkinson, we realised we still had another class match-winner in the side should Cunningham, Regis, Barnes or Ally Brown fail to find the net.

The idea for this book came from a series we were running in The Baggies newspaper, in which Tony looked back over his marvellous career. As a "serialisation in reverse", I decided that the material was so rich it merited publication on its own, so the three of us spent just three weeks developing the book you have in your hands. Not only does it tell a fascinating story of a basically one-club man — we believe the statistical material in the back of the book is unique; apart from the usual appearances and line-ups, we have dug out a description of every senior goal that Tony scored for the Albion (excluding friendlies and Testimonials, although they're all listed as well), which has never been done for a player in the top flight before.

We will never see another player spend twenty years of his playing career at the Albion — make the most of the story of a one-off, The Tony Brown Story.

Glenn Willmore
December 1998

Tony Brown played in more games and scored more goals for West Bromwich Albion than any other player. This book tells his story. He has always been one of my heroes ever since my Dad took me to my first Albion game at The Hawthorns in 1967. I was eleven then, and I was Albion mad. I'm 43 now and I'm still Albion mad. You can well imagine how much this book means to me!

I hope that it will bring back happy memories for all Albion fans who watched Tony throughout his great career. For those who missed him — then I hope it will give them the full flavour of those marvellous days when Albion were the premier Midlands team and Bomber was a star.

John Joseph Homer

ACKNOWLEDGEMENTS

The authors would like to thank the *Birmingham Post and Mail*, Geoff Wright at the *Express & Star*, Kevin Grice, Laurie Rampling and Dave Holloway for providing photographs for this book, Louise for proof-reading, Colin Mackenzie for details of Tony's appearances with Albion and Stafford — and William for being so helpful during its production.

"Pass to a blue and white shirt — and always beat the Villa!"

There are few greater ironies in the history of West Bromwich Albion than the one that occurred at Oldham Athletic on April 24th 1976. In the 55th minute the massed ranks of Albion fans who had invaded Boundary Park cheered in unison to acclaim another goal from "Bomber" Brown. Nothing unusual you might say, but this was not any "Bomber" Brown goal — this was SPECIAL. Albion's long hard season had reached its frenetic climax and two points at Oldham meant promotion.

That goal propelled Albion back where they belonged, back to Division One, the top flight, the footballing elite. Although it was one of many goals that Tony Brown scored in his time at the Albion, historically it was probably the most important one he ever blasted home — which IS ironic, really, because Tony was born, of all places, in Oldham!

Incredibly, when he scored that goal, Tony had already been at the Albion for fifteen years, and would still be there five years later, before bringing down the curtain on his Hawthorns playing career in 1981, by which time he would have laid claim to the title of "Mr Albion", with records galore under his belt.

Most appearances, most goals, most games at The Hawthorns, Player of The Year trophies, Cup winners medals and tankards, an England cap — the list is extensive. What a proud legacy for the lad from Oldham who supported Manchester United as a lad, could have signed for Manchester City — but ended up playing for West Bromwich Albion. Tony Brown (or should we say, Anthony Brown, as he was known in the Albion records until the arrival of another A. Brown at the club in 1971) was born in Oldham on October 3rd 1945. At an early age, he moved with his parents to Wythenshawe, Manchester where the young Brown spent his formative years.

One of three children (Tony has two sisters Veronica and Karen, who both still live in Manchester), Tony had no family connections with the professional game, other than his uncle, who spent some time as a reserve player with Grimsby Town just after the war. As a lad, he was

United daft, even though he only lived a stone's throw from Maine Road. On the terraces of Old Trafford, he would thrill to the exploits of the Busby Babes; they were his team and, no doubt, like all young boys who are enthralled by the game of football, it was his ambition to emulate his heroes.

"I used to play football for the school in the mornings, and in the afternoons I'd be at Old Trafford, in the Stretford End. I used to watch the Youth and the Reserve sides as well, along with three other mates, because in those days, if you wanted tickets for the big first team games, you had to collect programme vouchers, and they gave them out at second and third team games as well; but I missed the matches in 1958 against the Albion, and at Wembley, because I just couldn't get tickets."

Tony's love of United — and, who knows, his entire football career, had been kindled by his father, who took him to his first game at Old Trafford to see United play Bolton — Tony can still remember the impressive figure of Nat Lofthouse playing for the Wanderers, although his own early United hero was Eddie Colman. "He used to do some lovely shimmies. And there was Bobby Charlton just coming through. In the Reserves, I used to watch Johnny Giles and Nobby Stiles, both of whom I would later work with at the Albion" Later on, Denis Law would emerge as Tony's idol, so much so that even before he signed for United, and had been playing at rivals Manchester City, Tony would go to Maine Road to see his hero when United were playing away. "Denis was my real number one hero. I used to copy him, like all lads do with their footballing idols, and if you look at photographs when I was at the Albion, you can see me holding my cuffs in the same way as Denis did when I raised my arm after scoring a goal!"

At school he played for the local area team — South Manchester Boys, which is where Wythenshawe was — then Manchester Boys and the Lancashire County side. Only three of those young aspiring footballers made it to any sort of national football prominence. Tony — obviously — David Connor, also from Wythenshawe, who played nearly two hundred first class games for Manchester City and Preston North End, and Macclesfield-born Alf Wood, a big bruising centre-forward of the old school who was also picked up by the Maine Road outfit. He only managed a couple of dozen appearances for City, but went on to enjoy a long career in the lower reaches of the League, playing around 600 games, all told, for the likes of Shrewsbury, Millwall, Hull and Middlesbrough before ending his career at Walsall, just a few miles down the road from his former schoolboy team-mate Tony Brown. Indeed, the path of the two men nearly crossed again in 1974, when Don Howe tried to buy Wood for the Albion, from Millwall, but the burly striker decided that Hull City were a better option than West Bromwich Albion...

Tony had a problem with asthma, right from the age of three months up until he was fourteen. The breathlessness was a serious hurdle for a young footballing hopeful to have to put up with, and many a time it stopped Tony from playing, as well as causing him to miss his more academic pursuits for often lengthy periods, as the youngster suffered attacks which made it virtually impossible for him to breathe. “It was really bad; sometimes I just couldn’t go out and I was gasping for breath. And there was no real treatment in those days, no inhalers or anything. They just gave me a tablet at the hospital which you let melt on your tongue, which gave a bit of relief. I had to go to the hospital three times a week for breathing exercises, so you could say the illness affected my whole life. Many a time my parents would forbid me to go out and play football, but I sneaked out and came back hardly able to breathe — but I just loved football so much.”

Tony persisted with his game, and his doctor insisted that the exercise could only be beneficial for the ailment — it would “expand the lungs” — and at the age of fourteen, the condition “cured” itself leaving the teenager free to concentrate on football, rising through schoolboy ranks in the Lancashire county. As a fifteen year old, he was courted by Les McDowell from Manchester City, but a trip to West Bromwich, organised by Albion’s Manchester-based scout John Shaw changed Brown’s life forever.

“The asthma left me just before I joined the Albion, fortunately enough, because like many football-mad kids, I had nothing else planned if I hadn’t gone into football, and I joined the Albion as soon as I left school at fifteen, as you could in those days. I’d always wanted to be a professional footballer; that’s all I’d ever dreamed of doing.”

Manchester City actually offered Tony a professional contract, and he agreed to sign for them, but Shaw, who had been watching Manchester Boys for some time, arrived on the scene, visited Tony at home and had a chat and asked him to go down to visit the Albion.

“I told him I’d already agreed to sign for City, and he said, ‘You can come down with your father for the weekend and have a look around — it can’t do any harm’, because I hadn’t actually signed anything for City. So my father said ‘All right’ and we came down. There was something about the place — I just took to it straight away, the club, you know.”

Tony certainly made a good impression in his brief trial at the Albion. In a practice match on the old Revo ground in Tipton, which Albion used to use for training before they set up the new Spring Road complex, Tony scored a hat-trick. After the game, the party returned to The Hawthorns and informed Tony and his father that they wanted to sign the youngster and he put pen to paper, making Tony, not an amateur, as has been published in the past, but as an Albion apprentice professional, on April 13 1961.

"The Albion soon drilled football into you. There were a couple of rules they always told you. One of them was 'Always pass the ball to a blue and white shirt, and keep the ball on the floor' — that was always an Albion tradition." The other was another proud tradition that had been instilled in the club's players and supporters since the 1880s — "Always beat the Villa!"

Tony took the view that moving away from home and living in digs would help him grow up in a way that would have been impossible commuting between Maine Road and the family home in Wythenshawe. He moved to the Midlands almost immediately — living on the princely sum of £6 a week as his apprentice's wages from the Albion — and stayed in temporary accommodation next to future team mates Bobby Hope and Campbell Crawford in Camp Lane, within easy walking distance of the ground. Hope, in particular, soon struck up a friendship with the young Brown that has lasted to this day, and the two Scots were a great help as the Mancunian adjusted to life away from home.

That initial spell away from home lasted just four weeks, until the end of the season, when Tony was granted a quick return to the family home, but when the close season finished, the excited youngster returned to the Albion to take up digs near the Thimblemill, in Smethwick, in Alexandra Road, with an elderly couple who looked after him well for the three years. "Mr and Mrs Hunter were superb, looking after me and treating me like a son, making me very welcome and helping me to settle in a big way."

It wasn't just "at home" that Tony felt comfortable and well looked after. The Albion's treatment of young talent was second to none in the Sixties. "Wilf Dixon was great. He was the trainer, and he looked after all of us like a father. They had a very good youth system at the Albion in those days, and their scouting system spread all over the country. There was Graham Lovett in my 'year', and there was Campbell Crawford and Bobby Hope and Gerry Howshall before me, all very good players. Gerry, along with a lad called Mickey Fudge, were the ones, along with Bobby Hope, of course, who I thought would really make it big, because when I signed, the manager, Clark, was talking about Gerry being a future England international, but he faded away and after a few games in the first team, left for Norwich. But we were all there together, living and working and knocking about together in the same area. We lived near each other and we went in to the ground together on the bus and came back together on the bus, because youngsters in those days didn't have cars — of course, most of the first teamers in those days didn't have cars! We went away at the end of my first season, to the Youth Tournament that the Albion used to enter in Holland, and I remember that that was the first time I'd ever flown, in 1961, it was."

Albion regularly entered a side in the Blau-Wit Youth Tournament in Amsterdam, and had won the trophy on several occasions in the past. Tony remembers the trip well because the youngsters were forced to room with local families, almost like an exchange visit. "This family took me home from the ground, but the following morning I had to make my way across Amsterdam for training by myself. They told me the bus numbers, but I was completely on my own, in a foreign country, at fifteen. It was a miracle that I managed to do it".

Tony played his first game in an Albion shirt for the 'B' side at Birmingham City a couple of weeks after deciding to sign for the club, in a 5-1 defeat on April 29th 1961. In the July of that year he was confirmed as an apprentice professional, and the *Albion News* in August 1961 lists him as Brown, A, birthplace Manchester, height 5' 5.¾", weight 10 stone 4 lbs, previous club, Manchester Boys.

The 1961-62 season was his first at The Hawthorns. For Albion it was a transitional period. The great side of the Fifties had broken up, gentleman-manager Vic Buckingham had gone and his former assistant Gordon Clark was in charge. The senior members of the side were Bobby Robson, Don Howe and Tony's first Albion hero, Derek Kevan; it was ironic that for the first game of that season, the Baggies faced Sheffield Wednesday, managed by Buckingham, who had just moved to Hillsborough after a spell in charge at Ajax. The Owls won 2-0.

There was a fascinating documentary shot at The Hawthorns in this period, actually just after Clark left the club, called *The Saturday Men*, featuring some of Albion's big stars, like Derek Kevan, Don Howe and Bobby Robson, and Tony was on it — if you look carefully! "Just for a second. If you look at the bit when they pin the team sheets up on the wall, and a crowd of young lads all crowd round to read it, there's me!"

That posting of the team sheets was a ritual at the Albion in those days, as at all professional outfits. "On a Friday, everybody would be waiting in the dressing room and they'd put up four or five team sheets and you'd see where you were the following day. You'd be bitterly disappointed if you had been dropped from the team you expected to be in — and, I found, it got worse as the years went on. Half of your money was made up of appearance money, so if you were dropped from the first team, you lost half your wages. So the following week, you'd train like hell to try and impress the manager and get back in the team. That was your incentive not be dropped, and get back in the side. But anyway, apart from the money side of things, from a professional point of view, the first team was the only place to be."

The scene was repeated, writ large, at the end of every season, when the retained lists were posted in the dressing rooms. "It was terrible. You'd all be waiting one morning and everybody would be frightened to death. You'd see players literally shaking, dreading not being on that list. There'd be a clamour for the board, you'd all look and if you had been retained, the relief would be unbearable, unbelievable. I never got to the stage when I felt one hundred percent secure about being retained — and then, in the mid-Sixties, they changed the system, and abolished the ritual of the retained list, thank God!"

In those days, there was still a strict hierarchy at the club, with the professionals never mixing with the youngsters. "We never had much to do with the first teamers. They were a bit aloof then. Nowadays, there's all sort of banter between the age groups at clubs, but then it was strictly Mr Howe, Mr Robson, Mr Kevan. You only went into the first team dressing room to pick up their boots for cleaning, and if they told you to do anything, you jumped. Having said that, they were good to you as well, talking to you and advising you about the game."

One occasion that Tony does remember some social contact with those illustrious first-teamers was when his mate Campbell Crawford gave Tony and Derek Kevan a lift in his car. "We were lucky, then, as youngsters, because Campbell had an old banger, which was great, because in those days, I think only Bobby Cram, in the first team, had a car, and we used to get lifts in it except that most of the time, it ended up breaking down. One time, it broke down in Dartmouth Square in the centre of West Bromwich High Street, and we all had to get out and push it — and we had Derek Kevan, in his England blazer, helping us push this old wreck!

Tony Brown, apprentice footballer

Also in the first team at that time was David Burnside. Long before Tony had joined the club, back in 1957, a young Burnside had caused a sensation with his incredible ball-juggling skills which were featured on national television during the half time break of the Albion-Moscow floodlit friendly at The Hawthorns. Tony had been one of the many thousand of viewers of the live broadcast, and had been most impressed — or not! "I wasn't at the Albion when Dave used to entertain them with his ball skills, but I saw the 6-5 match against the Russians on television. He couldn't play. I'll tell you now, he was the greatest juggler in the world, but he couldn't play football. He was meant for the stage, not the football field!"

Off the field, Spring Road, a "super new layout for training", was almost ready to house the Albion's Warwickshire Combination side, whilst the Midland Intermediate League team continued to share the Revo Ground at Tipton. Spring Road itself would boast three dressing rooms, a gymnasium "the size of an aircraft hangar", a running track and an all-weather pitch. In such surroundings young Anthony Brown would start to learn "the game". Alongside him learning his new trade were several youngsters who were to become firm friends, some of whom who would accompany him into the first team, others who would fall upon the wayside at an early stage.

Posterity records that Tony continued his Albion playing career alternating between the Midland Intermediate League side and the Warwickshire Combination team — the latter side had to face local works teams who, no doubt, would take great satisfaction in beating the Albion — scorelines such as Albion 0 Netherton 3 were not uncommon. And not only pride was bruised — limbs were damaged as well, as Tony dodged tackles from welders, turners and the odd labourer or two! "They weren't youth sides that we faced — they were all men, and they used to kick us to death. Coming straight from school, I didn't know what had hit me the first few games. They used to rattle us; it really was a case of "men against boys", but it was a good grounding for looking after yourselves. They'd got the brawn, we'd got the skill, but you had to learn to look after yourselves; it didn't do you any harm, and it taught you to look after yourself, football-wise."

In the Intermediate League, Brown soon illustrated his uncanny gift for grabbing goals, his first coming in a 4-1 against Wolves on September 4th 1961. That side not only contained Brown, but also Rick Sheppard, Ray Fairfax, Gerry Howshall, Kenny Foggo and Micky Fudge. The younger Bomber also starred in Albion's FA Youth Cup ties against Heanor Town (7-1) and Peterborough United (6-0) before recording his first Albion hat-trick at any level in the Midland Intermediate League, in a 7-3 away win against Port Vale on October 28th 1961.

He followed that just seven days later with four goals against Notts County at the Revo Ground — Tony had well and truly arrived, and by the season's end, his goal tally was well over the twenty mark. Never was there a better time to be a young footballer; the maximum wage had been abolished, the Swinging Sixties were about to explode, whilst the Albion Youth set-up was second to none. Coached and tutored by the likes of Wilf Dixon and John Jarman, Tony approached the 1962-63 season full of optimism. Gordon Clark, the manager who had sold the club so well to Tony in the beginning, had left, really well before Tony had got to know him. "Funnily enough, he used to live near my first temporary digs in Camp Road, so for those four weeks I used to walk into the ground with him and have a chat with him, but obviously I wasn't involved with the first team, so you didn't see much of the manager. He was a nice fellow, and he was the one who persuaded me to sign for the Albion — he put the club over to me very well."

Archie Macauley was the new manager, his legacy in his brief spell at The Hawthorns being the fact that he was the man who sold Derek Kevan, the darling of the crowd, and a big early goal-scoring hero of the young Bomber. "When I first joined the Albion, I used to clean Derek Kevan's boots. I didn't see much of him, but he was a big hero for me because he was a goal scorer, and being a striker yourself, you obviously look to goal scorers. Derek was the big one at that time, and they didn't really have a prolific goalscorer after that, at least until Jeff (Astle) arrived in 1964. Kevan was a real star. His size, for a start, and he was a good looking lad, and always well groomed. I was always in awe of him — a real superstar." Big Kev's last match was in a 6-1 home win against Ipswich; the following game, he would sit in the stands at Molineux, as a Chelsea player, watching aghast as Albion were thrashed 7-0.

Around the same time, Kev's direct successor, had he but known it then, Tony Brown, was knocking on Macauley's door asking for a chance in the "stiffs". Although he continued to score regularly in the junior sides, Brown's aspirations for a Central League chance were ignored by Albion's dour Scottish boss.

"Archie Macauley followed Gordon Clark, but he was only manager for a very short while. I'd reached the age of seventeen by then, when you could sign pro, and I can remember constantly knocking on Archie's door, asking if they were going to sign me up, and he kept saying "Well, we haven't made our mind up son, you'll have to come back again", and I'd go back, and I'd get that story a few times."

Tony remembers that period as a depressing time — he felt as if he were "in limbo" with his future uncertain, as indeed, it was, dependent as it was on the whim of a manager, under pressure because of poor results in the first team, who probably had little time for the youths and reserves. Then Jimmy Hagan took over.

Hagan joined the Albion following Macauley's resignation in April 1963, significantly at the same time that Major H Wilson Keys stood down as chairman, after fifteen years, to be replaced by Jim Gaunt. Tony had been struck by the way the authoritarian chairman would sometimes come into the dressing room before matches. "Major Wilson Keys used to come in before the game and give us a team talk. He'd come in with his hat on and stand there. 'We're playing Everton. Who's the captain? Find out which way the wind's blowing. Kick with the wind in the first half, and kick the ball as far as you can in their half, and keep chasing it. Try and get a goal. All the best today, lads' Then he'd walk out, and the manager would say 'Take no notice of that!' It couldn't happen today, of course. No manager worth his salt would allow the chairman in before the game."

It was the new chairman who made it his duty to appoint Hagan, who had been a tremendous success at Peterborough. Hagan, in turn, recognised Brown's potential — and in the final Central League game of the season, Tony Brown made his Reserve team debut at The Hawthorns against, of all teams, Manchester United.

Albion lost 3-2 but Brown had the thrill of scoring a goal past one of his boyhood heroes Harry Gregg. Eddie Readfern netted the other, whilst Scot Max Murray played his last game in an Albion shirt, missing a penalty, in the following side: *Millington, C Crawford, Lovatt, Howshall, Campbell, Bannister, Macready, Brown, Readfern, Murray, Scarrott.*

Tony will always be grateful to Hagan for signing him up and, indeed, giving him his first chance in the Second and the First teams. But he recognised how difficult the man could be with his aggressive style of management, which had earlier come to the fore when, during the terrible winter of 1962-63, the senior players had threatened to come out on strike when the manager refused to let them train in tracksuit bottoms.

After some heavy coverage in the national press, that was all forgotten a few days later when Hagan was nearly killed in an accident at Albion's Spring Road training ground. Brown was not a first team quad player, but had been training at the same time at the senior players. "I was in the dressing room when he backed his car down the canal bank at Spring Road. Somebody came in and said 'The manager's down the bank, in the canal' and we all said, 'You're joking' — we thought it was a wind-up! But we all ran out, and looked down that steep slope, and his car was in the canal at the bottom. It had ended up upright, and some of the lads had got the stretchers that were kept in the dressing rooms and were carrying him up the bank. One of the ones carrying the stretcher was Tony Millington, the goalkeeper. They got him half way up — and he'd injured his neck badly — and Millington was puffing and panting, and Jim turned half round on the stretcher and said, 'Millington, you're not fit. You're blowing — get back Saturday for extra training!' Tony told me afterwards, 'I felt like dropping him back down the slope'. He was like that, Jim. But he was very lucky — he could easily have been killed. But he wasn't away that long, coming back with his neck in a brace, with Albert McPherson taking over for a short spell. I think Jim was a good spotter of players. he knew his players, and he let you express yourself, which, for me, as an attacker, was superb; he encouraged you to go forward and score goals. He had a real presence about him as well. Everybody stood to attention, almost, when he was about. Nobody larked about, because he was very stern. And his training was hard. You'd never see a ball about except for a full scale practice match, and it was lap, lap, lap, run, run, run. And that's what so many of the players resented about him, although I got on well with him."

At the beginning of 1963-64, the *Albion News* still records Brown as an apprentice pro — but now having reached 5' 6.½" in height, and he started the season in the Warwickshire Combination, at Sankeys (of Wellington), but by the middle of September he was playing in the Reserves once more, filling in for injured team mates.

On September 14th Albion Reserves beat Burnley 3-1 at The Hawthorns to go second in the Central League. Brown and Fudge both played in the side and the following week the *Albion News* commented: "A word of commendation to those two very junior inside forwards Tony Brown and Michael Fudge who find themselves playing in higher football than could be expected."

Seven days later, Brown scored twice at Saltergate in a 5-1 win over Chesterfield Reserves; Jimmy Hagan had by now had a chance to have a good look at the free-scoring youngster, and Tony thought it worth a word. "Hagan saw me play and I went to him and asked him, and he said 'Yes, we're going to sign you' and I was very pleased, because it's a lot of pressure off you. It was a two year deal, and I was pleased enough, but no sooner had I signed it than I was picked for my first team debut, at Portman Road, which was another great achievement for me. I can still remember coming in on the Friday morning for training and being told to go home and get my things ready because somebody was ill, Eddie Readfern, I think it was, and I was playing against Ipswich the following day. It was Wilf Dixon who told me I was travelling, and added that he thought I'd got a good chance of playing. I rushed home to get my overnight case ready, and I hardly slept a wink that Friday night, just thinking about the game. I was so nervous and the coach journey there was awful in those days."

On September 27th, Tony signed as a full professional and then with injuries decimating the club, he made his first team debut at Ipswich Town the following week. Albion's team was: *Potter, Howe, G Williams, Fraser, Jones, Simpson, Foggo, Brown, Fenton, Jackson, Clark*. The forward line represents one of the smallest the club has ever fielded. As regards the match and the result, the *Albion News* of October 10th takes up the story: "Last Thursday, October 3rd was Tony's 18th birthday. He signed as a full professional one week before and learned on the same day that with only a handful of Central League games behind him, he was to play in the First Team at Ipswich. The climax — the match was won 2-1. When his side were one down it was Tony who scored a magnificent equaliser." It was a good goal — and well worth recording, even though another three hundred first class goals were to be added to it in a marvellous career. Doug Fraser started the

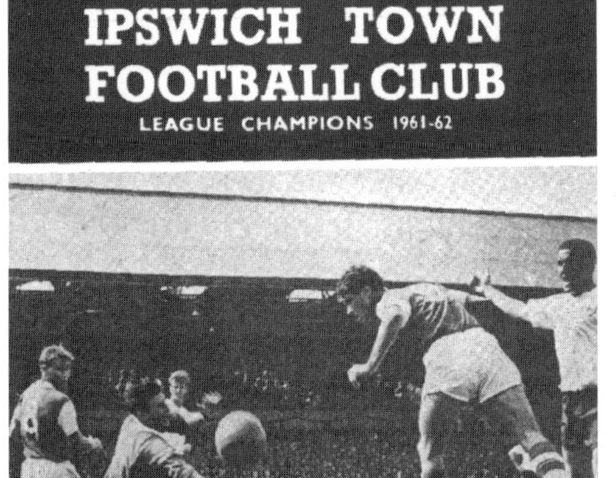

The Ipswich programme from Tony's debut game

Foggo, Brown, Fenton, Jackson and Clark: Tony makes his debut in the smallest-ever Albion forward line

move, with an excellent pass to Brown which the debutant reached near the by-line. He confidently beat two Ipswich defenders with a neat drag-back with his left foot before smashing an acute drive high into the net past the Town keeper Roy Bailey — a goal that was to have eerie echoes some fourteen years later!

"I'd managed to get word back to my family that I was playing, but I was surprised when I was changing before the game and this head popped over the big window in the dressing room at Portman Road — it was my Dad and uncle, who had made the trip down by train from Manchester. So I was pleased with that, especially with scoring as well. I had my leg pulled in the dressing room after, but the only words from the manager were 'Well done son'; but to get as much praise as that off Jimmy Hagan was the highest acclaim, because he never used to praise players; it just wasn't in his make-up. The journey back home was fantastic, and the following day, I was reading all the papers, 'Brown this' and 'Brown that' and 'New Star at Albion' — and then I was dropped for the next match, which brought me down to earth!"

Despite his goalscoring start, Tony was back in the Reserves the following week when Readfern returned, and whilst the first team were drawing 0-0 at Wolves, Brown lined up against the Liverpool Second XI at The Hawthorns. He was soon in the first team again, however, when Aston Villa visited on October 12th, and in a thrilling encounter, which Albion won 4-3, Tony scored again, on his home debut, along with Bobby Cram, Alec Jackson and Kenny Foggo, and played two more games, at Liverpool and at home to Stoke (both, unfortunately, ending in defeats) before returning to the life in the Reserves.

The Stiffs at the time were always good for a goal or two. During November 1963 they won 8-0 at Manchester City, and 4-0 at home to Barnsley, and Brown weighed in with the odd goal or two, but he turned provider at Ewood Park, where Eddie Readfern scored FIVE — and Tony set up three of them! In the FA Youth Cup, restricted to players under the age of eighteen at the start of the season, Tony was twice on target in the 6-4 win at Coventry, in an Albion Youth team that included Dennis Clarke, Graham Lovett and Ian Collard.

Tony's fine form did not go unnoticed and on November 30th 1963, the *Albion News* for the Reserve game against Barnsley proudly proclaimed: "Tony Brown was included in the England Youth squad for a special get-together on Monday last week, and now we hear he is to play for the side against the West Ham Youth team on December 10th. Congratulations to him — may this be the first honour of many."

In January, he celebrated by scoring the winner against Man United Reserves at The Hawthorns, the Reds including Nobby Stiles and Albert

Quixall in the side, and the 1-0 win took Albion to the top of the Central League, where they were fighting it out, ultimately unsuccessfully, with Aston Villa, for the club's first Championship since the Thirties.

It was February before Tony made the first team again, as he scored on the first of the month in a 3-2 defeat at Burnley, making it three goals in five games. He played in eight out of the next ten first team games, but his run was interrupted when he was once again called up for England Youth team duty. The England side took part in the UEFA European Youth Tournament in Holland, between March 25th and April 5th. Tony missed four matches in the League as England won the tournament, beating Spain 4-0 in the Final, with a team made up thus: *Springett, M Wright, Noble, Kendall, B Wright, Hollins, Redknapp, Knowles, Sadler, Sissons, Rogers* — but Tony failed to get a game in the tourney. He did, however, represent England Youth in a friendly against a Santa Cruz XI, scoring twice in a 6-0 win. The match was not designated a Youth international, so no cap was awarded, but Tony still has the silver cup awarded to him as Man of the Match.

On his return, Tony played in the final three games of the season, against Nottingham Forest, Sheffield United and Liverpool, scoring twice. As the season closed, his first team appearances numbered thirteen (5 goals) plus 18 Reserve games (13 goals).

Albion's 1964 pre-season took them to Holland, also. They lost 2-1 to Alkmaar (Brown came on as a sub) then beat ADO Den Haag 2-1, when Tony scored his first goal on foreign soil. The third game saw the Baggies triumph 1-0 at Ajax, and Brown's form was such that he realised another ambition at the start of the new League season when he played in the opening game at Old Trafford against his boyhood idols and against Denis Law, one of his favourite players. "A full house at Old Trafford! That was a real thrill for me, as a United fan. I used to follow them at all the home games, and a few of the away ones, when I was a lad, and although I had played once before at Old Trafford, for Manchester Boys, this was a packed ground, 52,000, and it was quite something to go there and play against some of my idols — Denis Law, in particular, was a real idol for me, so to play against them was fantastic. And I scored in a 2-2 draw."

The United match programme gave details of Old Trafford's new North Stand, but failed to mention Tony in the Pen Pictures, although it did list him as number eight in the line-up. The *Albion News* reported:

"It was a good fast game and the 52,000 spectators went away satisfied if not all of them were happy. We were one up — two one down — and ended two all. Scorers Tony Brown, who is, incidentally, from Manchester, and a Foulkes own goal." Another useful player made his

Tony, caught on the training ground in 1964

first League appearance in that game for Manchester United — one George Best. "Besty was the best player I ever saw. A fantastic player. And even as a kid, he was marvellous. Graham Williams came in at half time in that game, after trying to give Best a kicking for 45 minutes, and said, 'What do I have to do to catch that kid?'"

Tony then notched three goals against Sunderland the following Wednesday in a 4-1 win, the *Albion News* again shedding light: "The opening of the game did not prepare us for what was in store. Stan Jones put his name on the score sheet with an "own goal" for Sunderland. Clive Clark put us equal with a header but the night must go to Tony Brown who scored his first First Division hat-trick." The youngster was so excited that he ran back to his digs to ring up his parents to tell them the news of his first treble in big-time football!

It was to be the first of many memorable floodlit games for Tony. In his best run so far, he played in the opening twelve games, but strangely enough, he lost his first team place two games after the arrival of Jeff Astle. John Kaye moved to inside right and Astle took the number nine. Brown only played another five games that season, but whatever frustrations he suffered, it was Central League opposition that suffered as a result.

In his first game back in the Reserves, on October 17th 1964, Albion thrashed Chesterfield 6-1 —and Tony Brown hit a hat-trick past a certain John Osborne in the Spireites' goal. Two weeks later he scored four (two penalties) in a 7-2 home win over Derby, but with the first team boasting Kaye, Astle, Hope, Clark and the in-form Ken Foggo, Tony could not force himself into the reckoning, and it was at this time that he decided that perhaps it was time for a move.

"I asked for a transfer at one stage. I wasn't enjoying it because I was in and out of the side at the time. I'd scored a few goals, but I was a young lad, you know, and I went into Hagan's office and asked for a transfer — and the manager kicked me out! 'Don't be stupid, lad' sort of thing, and that was it, and it was all forgotten. Just a temporary blip, and a silly thing on my part." It was to be another eight years before the possibility of leaving The Hawthorns crossed Tony's mind again.

Rebuffed by Jimmy Hagan Tony settled down again and began to enjoy his football once more, and continued to score regularly, reaching a positive peak in April 1965 when he scored four times at Anfield in a 6-3 win over Liverpool Reserves. Seven days later, Bury Reserves were on the receiving end of another four goal blast from Brown as the Stiffs won 8-0.

Such form could not be ignored and thus the Bomber returned to the first team for the last two games of the season, scoring twice against West Ham in a 4-2 win on April 19th, and starring in a 1-0 win over Sheffield Wednesday in the last game. In those two games, Tony wore the number eleven shirt, thereby completing his forward line set! For the Stiffs, he had scored an astonishing 22 goals in 20 games.

When August 1965 approached, Brown could look forward to establishing himself at last as a first team regular. The Sixties soccer boom was about to start; for Albion and Brown the next five years were to be glory and goals — all the way.

League Cup winners in '66

At the end of the 1964-65 season, Albion travelled to South America and the youthful Tony Brown, still bubbling from his end of season recall, journeyed with them. He had, of course, been to Holland with the first team, but this trip was a foretaste of what was to come in the life of a jet-setting footballer at a top First Division club. But if that were not exotic enough, it was immediately followed by a trip to New York in July to take part in the New York International Tournament. Neither of these international jaunts are well documented, however, and for a flavour of "what went on" readers are advised to track down a copy of *Striker*, by Jeff Astle; his ever amusing anecdotes reveal an insight into those particular forays abroad by the Baggies.

Albion's first game in South America was in Peru, against Alianza Lima, on May 13th 1965. In front of a 20,000 crowd, Brown wasted no time in finding the net, heading home a Graham Lovett centre after just three minutes. Nine minutes later, Tony made it 2-0 when Lovett again crossed, Astle flicked on and Brown banged the ball into the net from five yards. Albion went on to win 3-2. Two days later, they met Sporto Cristal, winning 2-1 and once more Brown opened the scoring, cutting inside in the 35th minute to crash an 18 yarder into the corner.

Go west, young man — TB in NYC

Four more games followed, the tour ending on June 5th with the Throstles clinching a memorable 2-1 victory over Flamengo at the Maracana Stadium (in front of 30,000 of a possible 200,000 capacity) — heady days indeed. When the side were in Brazil, stopping in Rio de Janiero, they managed to get time off to play beach football on the famous Copacabana Beach, playing makeshift games against the local kids. The bare-footed youngsters regularly used to beat the professionals, using their great skills to keep hold of the ball and wear the Albion players out —- although they were all impressed with the power of Tony's shooting!

Tony had played his full part in the tour; indeed, he had so impressed the Peruvians in the first game that they had made overtures to Albion about signing him! The mind boggles at the thought of El Gringo Bomber; thankfully, for all of us in West Brom, it was not to be. "There was definitely an interest from the Peruvians. Jimmy Hagan said to me after the game, when I'd scored a couple of goals, that the local side had asked about me, and wanted to sign me — in Peru. A bit of a long way to go for a weekend, weren't it!"

From July 7th to 25th 1965, Albion played in the aforementioned New York Tournament. It was not an auspicious endeavour; they played six games in their group, winning only one, against Kilmarnock on July 18th (2-0). Tony failed to score in any of the games, and Albion failed to qualify from their section. If we are to believe Jeff Astle, then the most memorable tale from the whole trip is the Graham Lovett bidet story — perhaps another time, Jeff...

As anyone who has spent any time in New York during July will recognise, the city was hot, humid and uncomfortable to walk in — much less play a series of competitive games in. "For our training in New York, we'd be jogging round Central Park in those tempera-

Tony, front, relaxes on Rio's famous Copacabana Beach, with Ray Wilson, Clive Clark and Ian Collard

tures — over a hundred degrees — pouring with sweat, and we'd see the other sides, in the shade, just juggling the ball up and down, nice and relaxed. It was terrible, but to be fair, that's all the training we used to do in those days — just running round the track — we were all very fit, though. We never saw the ball, because they thought you'd want the ball more during the match if you never saw it during training!"

The tour ended with Albion needing a win against Polish side Byton in the final group match to qualify for an extended period in the city to play in the knock-out section. Albion crashed 6-0 — a result that Jeff Astle, for one, claims was not entirely a bad thing, so desperate were the side to return home!

Whatever the benefits of the tour, little under a month later Albion met West Ham on August 21st, to start the new domestic season. Having avoided any serious injuries on their travels, Jimmy Hagan could select his team from a full squad and, more importantly, perhaps, the players were fully fit and raring to go.

Off the field, there was a change in the coaching staff, with John Jarman, who had been quite influential in his early Albion career, leaving the club to become the Midland Area coach of the Football Association. The *Albion News* takes up the story: "Albert McPherson takes over from John Jarman. Albert considers himself a very fortunate man; twelve months ago he was a retired footballer, playing out his career in non-League. He was approached by the Albion and joined us as an assistant

Albion in their all-red strip, line-up for a pre-match photograph in Brazil. Back (l-r): Ian Collard, Stan Jones, Danny Campbell, Ray Potter, Ray Fairfax, Bobby Cram, Doug Fraser, Graham Lovett, Albert McPherson. Front row: Dick Krzywicki, Tony Brown, Jeff Astle, John Kaye, Bobby Hope, Clive Clark, Ray Wilson

trainer. His results with the Reserves recommended him for his present post." Albert McPherson was to be a highly influential "player" in the success of Albion over the next ten years or so. particularly with regard to the bringing on of young talent at the club.

For the Bomber, however, the start of the season was tinged with disappointment. He was left out of the starting line-up against The Irons, and travelled to Leeds Road with the Reserves. As the First Team set the standard for the coming season with a thrilling 3-0 win, Tony also got off to a great start, scoring twice in a 2-2 with Huddersfield.

The following Monday Tony visited his favourite "other" ground as the Reserves lost 1-0 to Manchester United, whilst on August 28th, when the First Team were losing 3-2 at Forest, Tony was at The Hawthorns netting a hat-trick against Sheffield Wednesday Reserves, in a 4-1 win. That particular game virtually ended the Bomber's career as a Central League regular — amazingly, in the next thirteen years, Tony would play only six Reserve matches, due to a combination of his consistent form and his continuing freedom from serious injury.

Clive Clark was injured in the home game with Sheffield Wednesday on September 4th, which let in Tony for the First Team game at Everton three days later, Albion winning 3-2 in a ding-dong encounter in front of 43,000, with Tony chipping in with a marvellous goal.

The next match at Northampton Town was memorable on two counts. Albion won 4-3 at the County Ground, and went top of the First Division. The *Albion News* recorded an historic first in the game: "Tony played on the left wing at Northampton, but in this match Ken Foggo was hurt before half

If it's Tuesday, it must be Argentina — the downside of foreign tours; those airport blues, as experienced by, left to right, Ray Wilson, Graham Lovett, Tony Brown, Dick Krzywicki and Danny Campbell

time and had to be taken off. During the interval it became clear that he was not going to be able to resume and we fielded our first substitute under the new rule by bringing in Lovett at inside forward, moving Tony Brown to the right and putting Bobby Hope on the left wing"

From this point, the Bomber became a first team regular — a position he was to cherish for another fifteen years — missing just two games all season, and he scored 17 League goals in 35 games, ending up just behind Kaye and Astle, who each scored 18. However, counting Cups as well, Tony was actually the top goalscorer at the club — because of Albion's first ever entry into the League Cup.

The League Cup had come into being five years before — at the start of the 1960-61 season — as an early season mid-week competition designed to milk the public's obvious enthusiasm for the new floodlit football, just as virtually all the League sides had erected artificial lighting for night games.

However, the competition, the brainchild of doughty Football League Secretary Alan Hardaker, had never really caught on. For one thing, the top clubs of the First Division, including the Albion, had treated it with disdain, and with one or two exceptions (Manchester United gave it a go in its first season) the big clubs refused to enter, so without the likes of United, Spurs, Arsenal and — yes — Albion, those clubs achieved some sort of self-justification. They would not enter it until it was taken seriously — and it would not be taken seriously until they made up the numbers.

Albion were the first of the top sides of the time to break ranks, when it was hinted that the 1966 winners, subject to their being members of the First Division, would be offered a place in the Inter-Cities Fairs Cup. At last, the League Cup had a carrot to offer the stubborn mules of the First Division — and how Albion were glad that they took up the offer!

The Throstles' first game in the competition was on Wednesday September 22, when neighbours Walsall visited The Hawthorns (for the first time in peace-time football for over sixty years!) and the fact that the attendance at an Albion-Walsall game set a new record for the competition (of 41,188) shows just how neglected the League Cup had got. In a very close game, Albion won 3-1. Stan Bennett put through his own goal to give Albion the lead, then Walsall equalised AND had a goal disallowed before Tony Brown, of course, popped up to score two late goals to send Albion through.

By beating Leeds United, Coventry and the Villa Albion progressed to the semi-final, a two-legged affair against Jimmy Hagan's former side Peterborough United — who, coincidentally, were managed by

Gordon Clark; the man who had taken Tony to The Hawthorns.

The first leg against the Posh was played at home. Peterborough arrived with a defensive formation, but took the lead through Vic Crowe. Tony equalised for the Albion with a back-header, and Astle scored a second in the 36th minute, but despite wave after wave of attacks, the score remained at 2-1.

In the second leg, Albion's attacking flair proved too much for the Third Division side and Brown well and truly made his mark on the competition with a superb hat-trick in a 4-2 win.

His first after 18 minutes was a close range shot, his second, after 57 minutes came from a Bobby Hope pass and his third was unselfishly set up by Clive Clark, leaving the Bomber with a tap-in; that made it 6-3 on aggregate, setting up a Final with West Ham.

Tony remembers that the preparations for the 2-1 first leg defeat at Upton Park were less than perfect. "The team coach broke down on the M1 on the way to Upton Park. There we were, stuck on the side of the motorway, when we managed to flag down a van. 'We're playing tonight at West Ham in the League Cup Final — can you give us a lift?' All the lads climbed into the back of this van — it was a big one — and we went to the biggest match any of us had ever played in in our lives in the back of a big van!"

Not surprisingly, Albion lost that game 2-1, but thrashed the Hammers 4-1 at The Hawthorns with an exhilarating first half display — four goals in 34 first half minutes — which most Albion men regard as the best game that they ever played in. In front of a crowd of 31,925. Brown scored Albion's second goal after 17 minutes, when Cram lobbed the ball over the massed West Ham defence and Brown got his head to it before Standen could reach it. The other goals came from Kaye, Clark and Graham Williams.

Tony will always remember that game. "I've always said that the second leg of the League Cup Final against West Ham was the best performance I've ever seen from an Albion side. That was the best team performance that I ever played in as well, and I played in some good games in the Seventies, under Ron Atkinson, with Cantello, Willie Johnston and Laurie Cunningham — great games, but that West Ham one was definitely the best ever. I've never played in a team that's been so wound up in a dressing room, as we were that night — we just couldn't wait to get out at them, and get the goal back, because we'd lost the first leg 2-1. We went out and from the first second, we absolutely destroyed them, Geoff Hurst, Martin Peters, Bobby Moore — they had a tremendous side, but we absolutely annihilated them.

Actually, I saw Jimmy Hagan (who, sadly, passed away in 1997) a few years ago, in Walsall. He'd just come back from Portugal, and we were talking about that Final, and he said, 'You'll always remember that match!' On the night, Jim didn't need to say anything, but he never used to say much before games anyway — the best game I've ever been involved in!"

The League Cup winners tankard was Brown's first major honour. In nine League Cup games he had scored nine goals, becoming the first player to score in every round of the competition — a feat that team mate Clive Clark would actually surpass the following year by scoring in every GAME, as Albion defended their trophy. In the League, Albion had finished sixth, with 91 goals, top scorers in the First Division, in fact. More importantly, that League Cup win, for the first time ever, gave them a ticket into Europe.

"We were a free-scoring side at that time, with a lot of goals in the side — myself, Jeff Astle, Chippy Clark, twenty goals a season each of us. We only knew one way to play, and that was to go forward. That was Hagan's philosophy — the best form of defence is attack — and he encouraged everybody to go forward. We always knew, especially at home, that if our opponents scored a goal, we were always capable of scoring two to beat them. It was like a cavalier style of football." That philosophy paid off well enough it the League Cup — but it also paid dividends in the First Division. The side was perhaps too cavalier for its own good over the marathon that is the First Division Championship, and it could never live up to its early promise that season.

All the same, there were some stirring games, particularly at The Hawthorns, as Fulham were beaten 6-2, Nottingham Forest 5-3, Leicester 5-1, Stoke 6-2 and Sunderland 4-1 at home and 5-1 at Roker Park, and an end of season run-in of just two defeats in the last sixteen games saw the club achieve a placing of sixth, its best League placing since the glory days of Vic Buckingham at the end of the Fifties.

In the summer of '66, England won the World Cup, Albion had won the League Cup, Tony Brown was top scorer at the club, Villa were in terminal decline and both Wolves and Blues were in Division Two. Good Old Days! Albion's legendary forward line of Brown, Astle, Kaye, Hope and Clark were looking forward to a Championship challenge and Europe in 1966-67.

On August 20th 1966 Albion visited Old Trafford for the opening game of the season, Back at The Hawthorns the club announced that Mitchells and Butlers had helped turn the "old refreshment bars into buffet bars". At Man United, one would have thought that the Baggies were under the influence — because after 21 minutes they were 5-1 down! That match set the scene for a torrid season, as they eventually lost 5-3.

"We still had a good side that season. I was a midfielder then. I'd started in the first team with a number seven shirt on my back, but I never played as a winger — I just liked to rove and look for goals, really, which was new in those days, as you 'should' have been an out and out winger with the number 7 or 11 shirt on. I can remember, in my early games, the crowd shouting "Get on your wing, Brown!" I could never play as a winger, but after that I was more of a midfielder, coming in late and making runs, which really was a new thing in those days. I don't know how we went from being a very good side in 1966, to nearly getting relegated in 1967 — you just can't explain it — you get these spells in football, and you can't work out the causes.

From Tony Brown's point of view, it was personally a poor start to the season, as he played the first seven games, but only scored two goals. He played in a 5-1 win over Fulham at home on September 10th, but then hurt his back — undiagnosed at the time, but probably a slipped disc — putting him out of action for two months, missing nine League games, a League Cup match — and Albion's first foray into Europe, a 1-1 draw at DOS Utrecht on November 2.

"I returned to the side after being out for two months, the longest I've ever been out — that was from lifting weights in the gym, which hurt my back. That was a worrying time for me, because I'd had a lot of trouble with my back, and I was very worried that I would ever be the same as I was before the injury. It was a disc problem and I've had a lot of problems with my back ever since, to this day, and it all started at that time. I used to go to the West Bromwich District Hospital three times a week and they used to put me in traction, all wound up and stretched out. It was really worrying and I used to think 'Will I come back?' because it was so bad that I couldn't bend, or anything, and that two months seemed a hell of a long time..."

Medical and physiotherapy facilities at the club at that time were very basic. "Tom Jones, the ex-Blues man, was physio then, and for every injury in those days, the remedy was either the heat-lamp or the old finger massage. We had a lot of injections, as well. They used to send us down the hospital on Fridays to have an injection. Sometimes they'd work, but you were never 100 percent right. But you were grateful just to be able to play. Much of the time, they were cortisone injections, and a recent PFA study has found since that cortisone can cause serious long-term problems. Dozens of times I played after having had cortisone injections in my ankles, knees and back — particularly my back, which was a problem that dogged me the whole of my career —

and that's why I've had to have a hip replacement. Apparently cortisone destroys the joints of players over the long term, and I'm sure that's what happened to me."

Brown did nothing by halves, and his recovery from injury (his longest ever spell incapacitated, incidentally) coincided with the second leg of the Fairs Cup game at The Hawthorns. Brown was restored to the side at number seven, and in the 13th minute, Albion were awarded a penalty when a defender handled a Bobby Hope cross. With regular penalty taker Bobby Cram out of the side, Tony stepped up to take his first senior penalty, sending a shot low to the right of the keeper.

Bomber scored his second with a header on 69 minutes and completed his hat-trick in the 88th minute after drawing the keeper off his line. Brown had accrued another record — Albion's first (and so far, only) Euro hat-trick, as Albion won 5-2, 6-3 on aggregate. John Kaye, in his *Sports Argus* column, recorded thus: "It was great to see Tony Brown in his best goal poaching form. He has been feeling rather despondent about the back injury which has kept him idle for so long. This hat-trick was just the kind of tonic that the doctor would have ordered."

Tonic was certainly what was required during the season. For most of it, Albion flirted with relegation. In one disastrous month, in February, Albion were thrashed 6-1 in Europe by Bologna (on aggregate), lost by a new club record FA Cup score at Leeds (5-0) and then suffered the ignominy of losing, as holders, the League Cup Final at Wembley to Third Division QPR!

Brown's first appearance at the Twin Towers was not a happy one. Albion, of course, led 2-0 at half time thanks to two goals from former Ranger Clive Clark — only for a Rodney Marsh inspired comeback which saw the Loftus Road side win 3-2. To this day, rumours of a half time dressing room fracas abound — but Tony insists that nothing happened. "A lot of people have said that things must have happened at half time, the manager must have said something, or whatever, but nothing like that went on at all. To be fair, Jimmy Hagan came in and said, 'You've done well, go out and play exactly the same as you have been'. So we went out, but Rodney Marsh turned it on a little bit and there was a debatable foul on our goalkeeper for the winner, and they won it. That has to be the second most disappointing moment in my career — and how terrible it was coming out down Wembley Way after the game, with all the supporters so disappointed; it was awful. Dick Sheppard, I have to say, had stud marks all over his chest — he got studded in the build up to the goal, and we all thought it was a foul, but it's one of those things that happen in football, and you can't do anything about it."

But Tony does offer a possible explanation of why Albion's hopes faded away so dramatically in the second half. "Jimmy Hagan took us down to Lilleshall on the Friday, the day before the Final, and made us play an exhausting full-scale practice match 24 hours before the game! Can you imagine that happening these days?"

Near the season's end, with just four games to play, Albion were only three points from 21st place and relegation. Brown had scored just eight League goals, three of those coming in the Boxing Day win against Spurs, which included his first League penalty, which he blasted past Irish international keeper Pat Jennings.

Albion, of course, staved off relegation by winning ALL of those last four games, against Liverpool, 1-0 (Astle), West Ham, 3-1 (Astle, Brown 2 penalties), Blackpool, 3-1 (Williams, Astle, Brown penalty) and, finally, Newcastle, 6-1 (Brown 3, Williams, Foggo and Clark), leaving Tony on 14 goals.

Once Albion were safe from the drop, Hagan got his marching orders from the Albion. It was a shock dismissal, despite the recent struggles, but there were huge sighs of relief from certain players when the chairman came into the dressing room on the morning of his departure to tell the players the news, but Tony, for one, always rated the man.

"Jimmy Hagan made some good signings, but he was the sergeant-major type, the disciplinarian, and I think things were very tense at the time. Jimmy Hagan was actually a brilliant footballer. A lot of our training in those days was practice matches against the Reserves, and if Jim saw you were having a bad time, he'd come over to you, pull you off and say 'Watch me, this is what you should be doing' — and you wouldn't get another touch after that, because he'd play the rest of the match! But I tell you what — most times, he'd be the best player on the pitch! He must have been a great player when he was in his prime; some of the things he used to do on the practice pitch — you just couldn't get the ball off him. I learned a lot from him as a young player, about running at players as soon as you received the ball, to make things happen."

It was Hagan's abrasive style that had meant the end for him, according to Tony. "If Hagan had mellowed a bit, I think he would have got more out of the team, to be honest; before Hagan left, he got a lot of the senior players' backs up, and the dressing room just wasn't right, because of things that had happened with his disciplinarian type management style, and the atmosphere fell away a bit."

But Albion had escaped, unlike their near neighbours, Aston Villa, and even though Wolverhampton Wanderers came up from Division Two that season, Albion were undoubtedly top dogs in the Midlands by the time the new manager arrived to take over during the summer of 1967.

Winning at Wembley

Season 1967-68 started with a new manager. Alan Ashman, chicken farmer, was plucked from Carlisle to take over the reins at the Albion. Who? The fans may well have asked, but whoever made the choice, it was an astute one. Few fans, though, could have envisioned the glory ahead when the season kicked off on August 19 with a home game against Chelsea.

"Alan Ashman came in, and turned the atmosphere round. He was the very opposite of Jim; very easy-going, very relaxed — and he made the players relaxed. He was a gentleman-type of manager, and the players liked him, that was the main thing. They knew he was genuine, a nice genuine fellow and an honest man, and all of the players wanted to play for him."

August turned out to be a particularly eventful month for Tony Brown. In the opening match against the Pensioners he had two perfectly good goals disallowed as Albion lost 1-0. The following Wednesday Albion travelled to Molineux to meet the Wolves. The Wanderers, under Ronnie Allen, had been promoted back to the top flight, and Albion were their first visitors of the season. A staggering 52,438 saw a goal-laded thrill-packed encounter, with Brown the centre of attention in respect of two incidents that helped decide the outcome of the game.

After only six minutes Woodfield fouled Astle and the referee gave a penalty. West Bromwich-born Phil Parkes proceeded to save Tony's spot kick — and so the Bomber recorded his second miss from the spot, following a similar *faux pas* against Southampton at the end of the previous season. As a result, Wolves led 1-0 at the interval, thanks to Ernie Hunt's goal. Ken Foggo equalised, but within a quarter of an hour, Wolves raced into a 3-1 lead with goals from Mike Bailey and Dave Burnside. With twelve minutes to go, Kaye pulled a goal back. In the last minute, all hell broke loose as Brown scored what is unquestionably the most controversial goal of his career. "In the last minute, this long cross came over, and I thought, 'I'm not going to reach this' so I dived and PUNCHED the ball into the net! I got up and went 'Goal! Yes!' and the referee took one look and pointed to the middle — goal! I couldn't believe it! Phil Parkes ran all the way back to the centre circle, jumped onto the referee's back and pulled him over, so the ref sent him off!"

Phil Morgan in the *Express & Star* saw it all: "Few Wolves supporters will remember such a dramatic finish on the ground as they saw when Tony Brown appeared to punch in the Albion equaliser to start a scene that ended with Phil Parkes, the 19 year old Wolves goalkeeper, sent off less than a minute from the end. His dismissal was well nigh inevitable. He was understandably disgusted that referee E Carr of Sheffield did not see Brown punch the ball past him, but when he vented his wrath on a couple of Albion players and Mr Carr, the official was left with no alternative" (Morgan was the Wolves reporter, so we may have a biased view — but the goal stood, and Albion rescued a point). A week later, there was no quibbling as Albion thrashed Wolves 4-1 at The Hawthorns; a fine way for Tony to celebrate his 100th League game.

The atmosphere may have been more relaxed with the new manager — but the players had to know where the line was drawn. "Alan was very easy-going, but you knew you could only go so far with him. He was very friendly and nice and upfront and a gentleman, but you knew that if you stepped out of line, you were in trouble. After the 3-1 defeat in the League Cup at Reading in 1967, he had us all in the dressing room at Spring Road and gave us a right roasting, and told us all to take a good look at ourselves, because we had really disappointed everybody.

I think that it sank in a bit, because it was the first time we'd seen him go from being such a mellow character, to the other extreme, because we'd let him down. And we thought, 'We shouldn't let this fellow down' — it was a right bollocking. He was very young at the time, and unknown really — nobody knew him — but his honesty came through, and he was a proper character."

Although Brown's form was good in terms of his midfield contribution, goals, for a while, were hard to come by — by September 1967, he had scored just four in 17 games. The drought went so far as to cause Ashman to drop Tony to the Central League side once more, just for a couple of games, and while he was there, he had his first experience of playing in goal. In the home game against Sheffield United Reserves, with Albion already a goal down, keeper Rick Sheppard was injured and had to go off. He handed the green jersey to Brown, who played the remaining 56 minutes between the posts, as Albion drew 1-1. It was to be the first of three occasions that Tony went in goal for the club — the other two were both for the first team, of course — and he never conceded a goal!

Tony was soon back in the first team routine. Over Christmas, Albion completed a memorable Double over eventual Champions

Manchester City, and the Bomber scored in both games, but by the season's end he had scored only five more goals, to finish with 11 from 35 games.

In the FA Cup, however, he netted four vital strikes as Albion went on to win the trophy. In the third round at Layer Road, he scored a penalty to earn the Baggies a somewhat undeserved 1-1 draw against Colchester. "Of all the Cup matches, I remember Colchester very well. We all thought we were out, when they scored a second goal right at the death, and the referee disallowed it for some reason that we don't understand to this day. John Talbut kicked the ball over the stand in disgust because he thought we'd gone, but we got a draw and took them back to our place and beat them at The Hawthorns. I scored a penalty in the first game; I hadn't actually taken many penalties up to that point, because Bobby Cram had been taking them, for quite a long time, but when he left, they were looking for a new penalty taker and I volunteered to take them — and carried on for the rest of my career."

There was more good fortune for Tony — and Albion — in the next round against Southampton at The Hawthorns. "Again, we were struggling, and I tried a speculative shot from all of forty yards, way out, but I didn't catch it right. Their keeper went down on his knees to catch it and it hit a divot and bounced up over his shoulder and into the net for the equaliser. Lucky — but you need that luck when you're on a Cup run, and that's when you start to think 'Everything's going for us — this is going to be our year'. That built up — the further we went, the more confident we became. The dressing room was brilliant and we believed we could beat anybody at that time. In the replay at Southampton, we won 3-2 even though we had to have Graham Williams in goal after John Osborne got injured. In those days, it was Graham who fancied himself as the substitute keeper in training, so it was he, rather than me, who went in — a really great result, that was."

An even better result, after Second Division Portsmouth had been eliminated in a nasty game at Fratton Park, was the elimination of Liverpool after three epic games. "We played Liverpool in the quarter finals, and they were a great side, with so many internationals, and after we'd beaten them over the three games, we all started to think 'If we can beat Liverpool, then this really is our year!' Those three games were really tough. When we had to go to Anfield for the first replay, not many people fancied us, but we plugged away and got a draw after extra time. The team spirit at that time was brilliant. I always say, if your dressing room isn't right, you're going to struggle; but we had tremendous characters in our side."

And, of course, in the semi-final, Tony scored the second goal at Villa Park when Albion beat Blues 2-0. "In the semi-final, Blues had more chances than us, at Villa Park — but they didn't put them in. They didn't score. Fred Pickering had three good chances to score, and I can't remember him ever missing that number of chances in a game before. I had a shot, and it came back for Jeff and he struck it in. I remember my goal like it was yesterday. On the edge of the box, on the right hand side, I angled the shot into the far corner; I'll always remember that, and the crowd erupting. After the game, it was marvellous, because it's every footballer's dream to play at Wembley. Ask any player, even today, and they all want to play in the FA Cup Final at Wembley."

Tony soaked up the atmosphere, not only at Villa Park, but that which permeated the whole of West Bromwich and the Black Country in the weeks before the Final against Everton. "Before the Cup Final, we were taken away for a break. The build-up to the final is great; the press is chasing everybody, they all want interviews and nobody wants to get injured. It's all a bit special. And the team hadn't been picked until near the end of the week, so you'd got all the doubt in your mind about whether you would play. "Am I going to play, am I going to be

Tony reaches the heights — scoring against Blues to send Albion to Wembley

on the team sheet?" No matter how big a star you may be, you're always worried. It's a nerve-wracking week, and you just want Saturday to come so you can get on the pitch. I can remember hardly sleeping on THAT Friday night; when you do sleep, you dream of scoring the winning goal and all that. Then there's the thrill of the relief when you finally see your name on the team sheet and you really know that you're actually playing. The morning of the game is almost as bad. You get up, have breakfast and go down on the coach to Wembley, which is when the butterflies really start in your stomach."

In the Final itself, Brown, by his own admission, had a quiet game — but picked up his winner's medal, thanks to best mate Jeff Astle's extra time strike, and fully appreciates the contributions of his eleven team mates that famous day. "John Osborne: An underrated goalkeeper, but a tremendous one. The best I've played with, he would come out to the edge of his box to collect crosses.

Doug Fraser: Converted from an attacking wing half to a full back.

Tony and Jeff Astle celebrate their FA Cup semi-final win at Villa Park with a post-match drink in the dressing room

Hard as nails, committed to the cause, but he could play as well. A good passer of the ball, a great inspiration, a shouter who kept everybody on their toes.

Graham Williams: If you weren't pulling your weight, Willy would be the first one on your back. A good captain, a good leader, a good full-back. Another one as hard as nails — the ball might get past him, but YOU wouldn't...

John Talbut and John Kaye: A tremendous twosome. Very strong, good in the air, both hard men, good central defenders who wouldn't let forwards play. I think that John Kaye was a better player as a defender, because he was a good reader of the game. You couldn't shirk around Yorky; you didn't mess around with him, because he'd give you some tremendous bollockings sometimes. They were both hard men, mentally and physically.

Graham Lovett: He had his accident, and had done well to come back. He did a great job in the Final, having been given the vital role by Alan Ashman of stopping Ray Wilson. He did it very well, because the full back was Everton's main attacking outlet from the back, one of the first overlapping full-backs of his day. But before he had his two car

Tony in action on the hallowed turf of Wembley in the 1968 FA Cup Final

accidents, Graham was a truly brilliant player; he could have been one of the all-time greats. He had skill, strength on the ball, power — everything. He was just unfortunate to have had his accidents. He'd have been an international regular for many a year, otherwise, I think.

Ian Collard: He was a bit unknown at the time, but he did a tremendous job in midfield — a great engine, as they call it nowadays. A good passer of the ball, a good left foot — a good player, Ian.

Jeff Astle: What can I say? My best mate in football. Goals, goals, goals, was Jeff — and he scored the winner, of course.

Bobby Hope: What a player! Absolutely brilliant. You made a run, and if Bobby had the ball, you knew it was going to come to your feet, or just in your path. Brilliant at changing play, he was one of the old

FA Cup winners 1968: one of two great sides that Tony has played in. From top, then l-r: Graham Williams, Tony, Clive Clark, Astle, Collard, Hope, Stuart Williams, Lovett, Kaye, Fraser, Dennis Clarke, Talbut, Osborne

time greats — and he was always available in the middle of the field if you were in trouble.

Clive Clark: What would he be worth today? Somebody who could score 15 to 20 goals from the wing? He was like lightning; faster than anything that moved, and good in the box, and really hard. He'd go for anything in the box, and throw himself at anything, but his pace was the thing — what pace! He didn't have a good Final, perhaps, but that was because Everton had done their homework on him; a tremendous player.

Dennis Clarke: Came on as a substitute in the Final, the first ever in the FA Cup Final; you can't take that off him. A good player in his own right, good defender, who had also been in the losing Final against QPR. A good set of lads who got on well together, and complimented each other. These sides come along now and again and fortunately we were there together."

There was hardly time for the players to enjoy the incredible reception they received back in West Bromwich, when hundreds of thousands lined the streets to see the team parade the Cup on the team coach as it drove from Birmingham through the streets of the Black Country. Even before it was known that the club were in the Final, a post-season tour of East Africa had been arranged — and postponed because of the Wembley date — and the players had to jet out just a matter of days after their Wembley outing.

Clock those embarrassed looks — Tony can't even face the camera — as Denis Clarke, Jeff Astle, Tony Brown, Ronnie Rees, Graham Lovett and Ian Collard are feted with flowers before the start of their 1968 tour game in Nairobi

It was a controversial tour. Albion were pitched against the national sides of countries like Kenya,

Tanzania and Uganda, who wanted to prove themselves against the FA Cup winners of England. "There were some hostile matches there. That's where Clive Clark ended his career; it was a horrific tackle, I remember, that did him. The player lunged at him, thigh high, from about twelve foot, through the air, caught him right across the leg — wallop! It was awful, and he was never the same player again after that.

We played this one game, in front of the Presidents of Kenya, Malawi and Uganda, I think, and it got so bad that they had to call on the President of the country we were playing in to get their players to calm down. They knew we were the FA Cup holders, and they thought that that meant we were the Champions of England, and they were desperate to beat us — at all costs.

The game got so bad that we all got ready to come off, the only time that I've ever seen anybody sent off TWICE for fighting, when Asa Hartford came back on the pitch again for a fight! Graham Williams, as captain, said 'Right, let's go' but Alan Ashman stood on the touchline and said 'Get back on, you're not giving in to these. Get at them and show them who you are!' So we went back on, and beat them!"

In terms of results, it was a successful tour, with three wins and three draws from the six games, but at what cost — Albion certainly never satisfactorily replaced Clive Clark, who played fitfully the following season before moving back to Queens Park Rangers, ending his career playing his football in America.

On tour again, in North America in 1969, Tony sports some cool shades as he relaxes on board ship with Dick Krzywicki, Ron Potter and Dennis Martin

Tony had a fine season in 1968-69, as Albion went so near, but so far from retaining the FA Cup winning the

European Cup Winners Cup, scoring 23 goals in League and cups. In the League, Albion were never a force. They missed Clive Clark's contribution — he only scored two goals in his 17 games for the club, and new signing Ronnie Rees was never an adequate replacement for the goalscoring left winger.

It was on the cups that Albion concentrated once more, although their flirtation with the League Cup was once more very brief, as Peterborough United gained some revenge for that semi-final defeat in 1965 by beating the FA Cup holders at London Road. An early exit also looked on the cards in the European Cup-winners Cup when, in their first match in the competition, the Albion went down 3-1 away to Belgian Cup winners Bruges, in another torrid atmosphere. "Bruges: That was a battle — The Battle of Bruges, in fact, they called it at the time. Jeff got a bit of a battering, and got concussed. He didn't know where he was, which was great, because it kept him quiet for once! I remember Jeff being carried off the pitch on a stretcher, and when I saw him after the game he wasn't looking too good at all. Asa Hartford scored the goal in the first leg which kept us in it. He always caused trouble, wherever we went around the world, did Asa. He always start the fighting, the riots or whatever, then you'd find him far away as he could get at the other end of the pitch!"

Back at The Hawthorns, the crowd were looking for blood against the Belgians for their treatment of Astle, and Graham Williams had to appeal to the Brummie Road crowd to stop them from pelting the Bruges goalkeeper with coins. Astle still came in for some terrible treatment, but young Asa Hartford became the youngest British goalscorer in European competition when he pulled a goal back before the Bomber scored the goal that put Albion through to the next round on the away goals rule.

The trouble didn't stop there. In the next round, Albion travelled behind the Iron Curtain to meet Dinamo Bucharest, the state-funded team of the brutal Rumanian Securitate. Albion drew 1-1, but the problems started in the second half when Ronnie Rees was sent off for retaliation, after some tackles had been flying in. At the end of the game, the Albion players were pelted with everything that the crowd could get their hands on, and they had to be thankful for the action of the home players, who formed a human shield around them, to help get them off the pitch in safety. There was no problem in the second leg, when Albion completed a 5-1 aggregate against the Rumanians, Tony scoring two of the goals.

When Albion were paired with Dunfermline in the quarter-finals, the dismal record of Scottish sides against their English counterparts in

Europe meant that Albion were strong favourites to progress, but it was not to be. After a solid goal-less draw at Firs Park, Albion crashed in the second leg at The Hawthorns, in some of the worst conditions ever seen on the ground, with the Arctic wind blowing sand into the players' faces, already numb from the extreme cold. "The second leg was played in the coldest conditions I've ever played football in! It was the only time I've ever played in gloves; Alan Ashman sent kitman Dave Matthews out to get some gloves for all of us. We missed a few chances, and I had a goal disallowed and we lost 1-0, and went out."

There was still the FA Cup to defend. Right to the semi-final stage, it looked as if there would be a repeat of the previous year's Final. Tony scored some important goals in the Fifth Round against Arsenal, and the Sixth Round at Chelsea. "The key match was at Chelsea in the quarter final. I scored one of the goals in a 2-1 win at Stamford Bridge, but Bonetti saved my penalty kick, which I didn't catch right. But the atmosphere in that game was a bit nasty. I remember at the end when everybody was going in on John Osborne in the six yard box... Chelsea had some tough characters, like Chopper Harris. He was a hard lad, but you expected it in those days, because everybody had hard men like that. They could tackle you from behind in those days, as long as they got the ball, very different from now."

The FA Cup semi-final against Leicester at Hillsborough rates as one of Tony's greatest disappointments. A late Allan Clarke goal dumped Albion out of the competition, denying them a record-breaking third consecutive Wembley Final — and Everton missed out as well, losing at the same stage to Manchester City, who went on to beat Leicester in a disappointing Final.

"We were the favourites, especially as Leicester were relegated that season. We all thought we were going to win it, we all thought we were at Wembley again, and Graham Lovett had ordered a new car on the strength of it. He'd ordered it, a new Rover, on the strength of getting to Wembley! We were firm favourites, and confident, but we didn't play on the day. Allan Clarke scored the goal near the end, and that was another of my major disappointments. It was funny with Graham, though — the Monday after the semi, he returned to the showroom and when he walked in the door, the salesman said 'You want to cancel that car, don't you?'"

All told, Albion played 55 competitive games in '68-69, and Tony missed just one, in the FA Cup at home to Norwich (and, of course, were awarded a penalty in THAT game as well, but this time Astle put it away!) Tony was therefore and "ever-present" in the League for the first time, and he netted 17 goals — second to Astle's 21 — and his all-round play was rewarded at the end of the season as the *Albion News* duly recorded on April 23 1969.

"Tony Brown has played in everything but one Cup tie — Norwich City wasn't it? Tony had some special reward when he was chosen to be *Midlands Footballer of the Year*, to receive the Birmingham Mail Trophy. Jeff Astle continues to press his international claims. He is in Friday night's game, England versus Young England in London, and Tony has to go along as reserve for one of the sides."

Tony was actually presented with the Evening Mail-sponsored trophy before the game against Manchester City on Wednesday April 16. The England v. Young England fixture was played at Stamford Bridge two weeks later and Astle turned out for England whilst Tony Brown played for the Young England side. The result was 0-0 — but Brown had international recognition at last, a fitting reward for such a season of progress.

John Kaye in his *Sports Argus* column had the final word: "Tony Brown takes the very deserved limelight in being nominated as *Midlands Footballer of the Year*. It could not have happened to a nicer chap."

Wembley once more

In the summer of 1969, Tony had arranged a Match of The Day of his own, as, in July of that year, he married Irene, who he had first met at a night out at the old Manor House in Stone Cross, at St Mary's Church in Wednesbury. Tony's best man, of course, was his striking partner, Jeff Astle. Now, nearly thirty years on, Tony and Irene are still happily married, with two boys, Paul, born in 1977, and Adam, born 1981. Both sons are Albion supporters, of course, but their leisure time is taken up by their strong love of golf, rather than football.

As Albion fans would say, a marriage made in heaven — Tony and Irene, that is; Jeff was just Best Man!

As the Sixties drew to a close, Albion could look back on a period of unprecedented success in both the FA and League cups — but the club had even higher ambitions. Cup success was all very well, but Chairman Jim Gaunt was desperate for the championship to come to The Hawthorns for the first time in half a century. So much so that the board relaxed the traditionally tight purse strings at the club to allow an Albion manager the rare luxury of a splash in the transfer market, which took place in the summer of 1969.

Two of Tony's Cup-winning colleagues departed to make way for the new men. Clive Clark, an outstanding servant to the club throughout almost the whole of the Sixties, left to join Queens Park Rangers in a deal which saw Allan Glover, a 'teenage prodigy' with just a handful of first team appearances to his name, move north from Loftus Road.

Ian Collard, always a "nearly man", and a utility player of great versatility, went east to join Bobby Robson's Ipswich. Once again, a player-exchange was involved, to lessen the financial blow, as Ashman acquired the services of gifted Irish midfielder, Danny Hegan. "Danny obviously had problems in his personal life, and he'd go missing for days at a time. He was a very talented player, but you can't condone that sort of indiscipline at a football club for very long, because it affects the dressing room spirit pretty quickly. It was obvious Danny wouldn't be with us very long."

The third incoming name in that hectic few months was Colin Suggett. The youngster had an excellent scoring record at Sunderland, and Ashman had been talking to him for several months in an effort to persuade him to move south, but the club had to dig deep to get him, making him Albion's first £100,000 signing. "Colin was another good player, with a great touch and good vision, but he was in and out of the side after making a good goal-scoring start in 1969. He actually played better after he was converted to midfield later in his career. He used to come in the dressing room in a morning with the *Sporting Life* under one arm, and the *Pigeon Gazette*, or whatever it was, under the other!"

As it was, the signings failed to galvanise the side — not least because they were hardly used. Suggett was a useful foil to Astle up front, playing in every game and finishing as second top scorer, behind Astle and ahead of Brown, but Hegan was a disaster, a disciplinary nightmare who only played in thirteen games. Glover looked promising, but his youth and inexperience in the top flight meant that his full debut was delayed until almost the last game of the season. Once again, it was left to the old stagers — Astle, Kaye, Fraser, Talbut and, of course, Tony Brown, to carry the torch throughout another season dominated by a great cup run. "The players at the Albion had always thought that if the club had splashed out a little to buy a few more quality players, they could be challenging for the Championship, so we were very impressed when they bought Suggett, Hegan and Glover — but it just didn't work out."

For Tony, the season was something of a disappointment after his goal-scoring exploits of a year before. Undoubtedly, at the start of the campaign, he missed the dominating presence of Astle, out for seven of the first eight games because of a combination of injury and a dispute with the club over wages. Suggett was paired with the raw talent of reserve striker Percy Freeman, and started well with two goals in a 2-0 debut win at Southampton on the opening day.

That, unfortunately, was one of just two wins in the first fifteen games. Tony netted his first goal of the season on August 23, in a 3-1 win against West Ham at Upton Park, but it was on one of his favourite grounds, Roker Park, Sunderland, that he reached an important personal milestone. Captain for the day Suggett equalised an early goal from Dennis Tueart, only for Bobby Kerr to give the struggling home side the lead once more. Six minutes from time, up popped Brown to win a point, with his hundredth goal in first class football for the club. The *Sports Argus* described it thus: "With six minutes left, Albion snatched the goal they wanted. Krzywicki's speed won him the ball on the right and Brown nipped in to turn his centre into the net."

Injuries had not helped Albion's stuttering start to the season. With John Osborne injured in the first game at The Dell, Ashman had to turn to rookie keeper Gordon Nisbet to keep goal for the first time at Coventry. The youngster had a terrible debut between the sticks in a 3-1 defeat — but, curiously, he later gave up his goalkeeping role to try out first as a centre-forward, then as a full-back, at which position, amazingly, he later won back a first team place.

As a priority, though, Ashman needed an experienced goalkeeper as understudy to the always injury-prone Osborne, and he signed Jim Cumbes from Tranmere for £35,000. "A good keeper, Jim, but he was never as good as Ossie, who I've always thought was the best goalkeeper I've ever played with at the club. The thing with Ossie was that he'd come out for crosses, which was a great relief for central defenders, who didn't have to worry about it."

There was a boost when Astle finally returned to action — heralded by the broadcasting of the soundtrack of his Wembley goal over the PA system before the home game with Ipswich — and he struck with his first two goals of the season, even though returning Baggie Ian Collard helped spoil the occasion somewhat with a goal against his old colleagues in a 2-2 draw.

For once, it was Albion's home form, usually so reliable, that was causing problems. By the end of October, they had won three away games, at Southampton, West Ham and Crystal Palace, but had still not won at home. One memorable game at The Hawthorns in that spell was in front of the BBC *Match of The Day* cameras against Liverpool on September 27, when it looked as if the problem had been solved. Albion were leading 2-1, with the win "in the bag" until referee Keith Walker added six minutes of unwarranted injury time, allowing Roger Hunt to score a 96th minute equaliser. In the subsequent pitch invasion, the referee was assaulted by irate Albion supporters and the club was somewhat fortunate to be exonerated by an FA enquiry.

By this point, Tony's form had dipped to the extent that he was dropped for a couple of games, against Arsenal and Leeds (both finished 1-1). They were the only League games that he was to miss all season, and by the time Manchester United visited The Hawthorns on October 4 he was back in the side and raring to go against his 'favourite' side. There was more crowd trouble in the 45,120 crowd, with several Manchester United supporters being ejected from the Birmingham Road end of the ground before the game.

As usual, for matches involving Albion and United, it was another classic game, which looked to be going the way of the form book when Brian Kidd scored in the 22nd minute after Bobby Charlton had headed against the post. But Albion's reply was immediate. Albion surged forward from the restart and Ian Ure was adjudged to have handled the ball in the area. Tony stepped up to take the penalty, looking forward to yet another goal against his beloved Reds but Stepney, diving to his right, made a brilliant save. with Asa Hartford, with the goal at his mercy, firing the rebound at the keeper's legs, and out. It was doubly unfortunate that Tony should miss that penalty — it was to be the only one awarded to Albion all season!

Five minutes into the second half Tony made amends. "After fifty minutes the ball ran out to Brown on the edge of the box. His first time drive hit Astle, who was unable to get out of the way. The ball rebounded to Brown who again hit it with tremendous power into the top corner of the net, leaving Stepney helpless".

Inspired by that brilliant goal, Albion pushed forward and eight minutes later a rare goal from Bobby Hope clinched a customary victory against United, in a match also notable for a marvellous debut performance from a 17 year old defender, Alistair Robertson. "You could see right from the start that Ally was going to be a first team regular. He was always one hundred percent wholehearted, and never let you down. He wouldn't let centre-forwards play, he'd kick them, let them know who was in charge, and he was a leader and an organiser on the pitch."

By the end of the year, Albion's League form had settled down, and it was clear that there would be very little change from the Albion of old. Indeed, with Everton and Leeds streaking away at the top of the table, it was clear that there would be no League Championship for Albion — and, anyway, in the League Cup, a fourth Cup Final in five years was already beckoning!

Wins over Aston Villa, Ipswich, Bradford City and Leicester had taken the side through to a two-legged semi-final against Second Division Carlisle United. The first leg at Brunton Park resulted in a 1-0 win for the home side. The second leg was staged at The Hawthorns on Wednesday December 3 and the 30,000 crowd, fully expectant of brushing aside Alan Ashman's old club, were given a nasty shock in the first half, when, with the scores still level, Bob Hatton hit the Albion post when it might have been easier to score. A two goal lead would surely have seen the Cumbrian side at Wembley, but Albion rode their luck to score second half goals through Suggett, Hope, substitute Dennis Martin, and Tony Brown, who lashed in a tremendous free kick given inside the penalty area after the Carlisle keeper had broken the old "four steps rule".

With one Wembley ticket, against Manchester City, booked for March, Albion opened the new year looking for a another trip there in the FA Cup. For the second successive FA Cup tie, Albion travelled north to Hillsborough — this time to meet the home side, Sheffield Wednesday, who were struggling in the nether regions of the First Division, and who would be relegated at the season's end.

Albion fielded a weakened team — Astle and Hope were both out — and Wednesday triumphed with two goals from Jack Whitham in a game remembered for two incidents.

In the 82nd minute, with the score at 1-1 Colin Suggett, well onside, broke clear on goal, with only Springett in front of him, only for referee Smith to blow for offside, even though his linesman had not flagged. Apparently, the referee had seen the movement of a matchday steward's fluorescent coat, and confused it with the linesman's flag. John Kaye described the moment: "I protested to the referee and he immediately admitted he had made a mistake, and held his head in his hands. From the free kick Wednesday began building up the pressure that lead to their late goal" — although, to be fair, it has to be said that it still took a monumental mix-up between John Osborne and John Talbut to let in the sucker punch five minutes from time!

More notable, however, was the Albion goal, as of all Tony Brown's 307 goals for the Albion first team, this was the one he — and most surely the millions also watching on *Match of The Day* — would class as the finest of all. The *Sports Argus* reporter takes up the story. "All that had gone before was forgotten when Brown scored a magnificent equaliser in the 61st minute. The goal stemmed from a clearance kick from Osborne, who gathered a Talbut back pass. Martin met the kick perfectly, hooking the ball on to where Brown was waiting. The wing half turned and hit his shot instantly from the edge of the box to beat

Springett all ends up as the ball thrashed into the corner of the net." The goal was used for several years in the *MOTD* credits whenever FA Cup Third Round day came round, and was almost certainly one of the best goals ever recorded by the programme. Tony had few doubts about it; "It was definitely the most spectacular — the best — I've ever scored. It wasn't the most important, obviously, because we lost the game, but I took it as well as any goal I ever scored. I know that if I'd have gone back to Hillsborough and tried to have set up that goal to repeat it, I could have tried it a million times and never done it again. A real goal in a million — but it's nice now when ex-players say it's the best goal that they've ever seen"

It was back to the League for Albion — but the players still had the League Cup Final to look forward to. In late January, Manchester City came to The Hawthorns for a League Cup rehearsal and 30,000 saw Albion completely dominate the match and record a 3-0 win. Jeff Astle was on top of his form and, watched by the England selectors, thrilled the viewers of *Star Soccer* with a goal of supreme quality. Tony Brown, for once, was the provider: "Brown went racing free down the right wing, but when he centred Astle seemed to have little chance of a goal, but he controlled the ball knee high and spun around to beat Booth and Connor. He then lashed a tremendous drive into the bottom of the net past Mulhearn's right hand — a goal that deserved to book him a ticket with England in the Mexico World Cup".

Tony Brown remembers the game for a different reason. In the 32nd minute, Osborne was injured in a clash with City captain Mike Doyle. The Albion keeper carried on for five minutes but had to be lead off the field for treatment — and it was Brown who went in goal! He was immediately in action, saving a fierce drive from Young, his ordeal lengthened by a referee who added six minutes of injury time, which meant that Tony kept goal for a total of sixteen minutes before Ossie returned for the second half. Another clean sheet for the Bomber!

With the players obviously thinking of Wembley, League form dipped, with just only one win the next five games, culminating in a ding-dong encounter the week before the Final at home to Wolves, in which Albion showed their fighting qualities to come from behind three times in a cracking 3-3 draw.

If only the side could have shown those qualities a week later, in the League Cup Final. But Tony's third — and last — appearance in Albion colours at Wembley Stadium ended in disappointment. By his own admission, Tony had a quiet match, and can remember little about the game, apart from the early Albion goal and the state of the pitch, churned up by the recent *Horse of The Year Show*.

"Jeff scored after five minutes or so, but I remember the conditions more than anything. It was so muddy, you sank six inches into it, and if it hadn't been the Cup Final, it would never have been played, because you couldn't left your feet out of it. Franny Lee had a great game, but he'd got powerful legs and he ploughed through the mud. He turned it on, on the day, and he was superb, and we lost another Final. Four Finals in five years, which is some feat in itself, equal to anything that people like Manchester United do nowadays — and the season we missed out, we got to the semi-final, so it was so nearly five in five. That took some doing — you've got to be a good side to do that; a tremendous team spirit carried us through."

So Tony picked up his second runners-up tankard (The League Cup had to be different — they gave tankards rather than medals!) in a match that Albion, pre-match favourites for once, would have won but for a dreadful miss by Colin Suggett when Albion were still a goal ahead. Doyle subsequently equalised and in a gruelling period of extra time Glyn Pardoe scored the goal that would send the League Cup — latter followed by the European Cup Winners Cup — to accompany the FA Cup in the Maine Road trophy cabinet.

With the League Cup, and European qualification lost (although Albion held out the forlorn hope of a back-door route into Europe if City won the ECWC) the season wound down in meaningless fashion, although Tony's late flurry of five goals in the last seven games presaged something of the goal flood that was to come the following season.

In the post-Final losers' banquet, chairman Jim Gaunt reiterated his desire for League success — and that he was fed up with cups — in a speech that must have haunted him for years, as that trip to Wembley was to be Albion's last for over twenty years. It must have been almost as galling for Gaunt to have to take his side to Goodison Park — on April Fools Day 1970 — for the match which Everton gained revenge for a shock Albion win earlier in the season, to enrapture their 58,000 fans locked in as they clinched the Football League Championship. The trophy was presented to the Toffeemen after the game, and they paraded it around the packed ground, watched enviously by the Albion players — it was to be the nearest that Tony Brown ever got to the magic piece of silverware! "There was a lot of kidology in that match. Everton were so confident of winning that game, because they'd had a great season — but they brought a crate of champagne into our dressing room BEFORE the game!"

There was worse to come. In the penultimate game of the season, Tony accompanied his Albion team mates to Old Trafford as the "old man" of the side. With Williams, Kaye and Talbut all out, in favour of youngsters like Robertson, Hartford, Merrick and Lyndon Hughes, the average age of the side was just 23. But "you don't win anything with kids" — and Albion crashed 7-0. It would be another seven years before Brown was on the receiving end of such a thrashing again! "Of course, I remember that so much because it was at Old Trafford. Alan put Lyndon Hughes at full-back to mark George Best, who absolutely annihilated the lad, and gave probably the best performance from a player that I've ever seen in my career!"

There was still time that season for Tony to add to his overseas travels with the Albion, as the club competed in the new Anglo-Italian Tournament — and he notched two goals in the competition in Albion's only win in their four games, a 4-0 win over Italian Serie A Champions AS Roma. More memorable — for all the wrong reasons — was the game in Vicenza, which was the only goal that Tony played in which was abandoned for crowd trouble. "The match in Vicenza was terrible. Asa Hartford started all the trouble, as usual, the way he did all over the world! One of their men chased Asa the whole length of the field before diving on him at the end; Asa ducked and the chap went full length as Asa dashed into the dressing room and got away from all the trouble. Back outside, the fans were climbing the fences to try to get to us, and if they had succeeded, I think they would have lynched us. It was terrifying, the most scared I've ever been in a football match. We were kept back hours after the game, and then they revved the team coach up, suddenly opened these big gates and shot out — and they were all there, throwing everything at the coach. They were like wild animals."

When the long drawn out season finally came to its weary end — domestically, at least — Jeff Astle, Brown's strike partner and buddy went off to Mexico with England for the World Cup Finals, acknowledged as the top scorer in the First Division. When he returned, things would never be the same for either Astle or Brown. The King had begun the downward spiral in his career — whilst the Bomber would go on to take the spotlight and enjoy his best-ever season!

Tony Brown, England International

By the time the pre-season preparations had begun for the Albion in August 1970, Jeff Astle had returned from his World Cup adventure, and Albion supporters were expecting great things from the mature Brown-Astle partnership. Astle had already chalked up his hundredth League goal for the club, early in the previous season, and if Tony managed to maintain his excellent scoring rate (for a midfielder), he would be expected to reach the same milestone within the next couple of years. Events were to prove everyone wrong, as Tony embarked on the most memorable season of his career, goal-wise — a season that was to bring him to the pinnacle of his profession, as a full England international.

Goalscorer turns goalstopper at Blackpool!

The Albion squad had changed little over the summer, with the only significant departure being that of the wayward Danny Hegan, who had left for Molineux en route to a career coaching at that other holiday camp, Butlins. As regards new signings — the frantic activity of the previous summer had obviously exhausted the Albion purse — there were none.

The season opened well enough, once the side had got over the shock of only drawing at home to perennial strugglers Crystal Palace. Tony opened his account with a couple of goals in a 3-3 draw at Nottingham Forest, which saw the team come back from 3-1 down, but in the next game, against newly promoted Blackpool at Bloomfield Road, he once again was given the opportunity to see the goalscoring game from the other side.

Astle had given the Albion a first minute lead, only for the Tangerines to fight back. By the interval, they led 3-1, with the ex-Birmingham City centre-forward, Fred Pickering, who had gone so close to ending Albion's Wembley dreams in the 1968 FA Cup semi-final, taking some sort of revenge with a couple of well-taken goals. Early in the game, goalkeeper John Osborne had been injured in a mid-air collision with Bill Bentley, and thirty five minutes from the end, he had to limp off for good — and Tony grabbed the green shirt and went in goal once more. It was his third experience between the sticks, and once again, he managed to keep a clean sheet — and must surely go down as the only Albion goalkeeper in the their history to play in goal in as many as three games without conceding a single goal!

The team bounced back at The Hawthorns the following Wednesday when Stoke City were the visitors. One of Astle's colleagues from the Mexico trip, the great Gordon Banks, unquestionably the greatest goal-keeper in the world at that time, was in goal, and Tony had the pleasure of beating the great man twice. He particularly remembers one of the goals — a stunning free kick. "One goal which gave me particular satis-faction I remember, was when we played Stoke City under the Hawthorns floodlights. I always preferred to play matches at night, and when we were awarded a free kick about 25 yards out, I just hit it with everything towards Banks' goal. It went in like a rocket and the night atmosphere helped the ball to swerve away from the goalkeeper. Gordon spoke to me after the match and told me he never even saw it!"

At the end of August, with the supply to the front runners drying up a little, Ashman signed winger George McVitie from Carlisle. An appren-tice under Ashman at Brunton Park, he had reminded the former Carlisle manager of his abilities in the two legs of the League Cup semi-final the previous season, and was an inexpensive option to give the team a little more width.

McVitie made his debut at home to Newcastle on September 2 — and Albion suffered their first home defeat in nine months, despite Astle hitting his sixth goal in as many games. The Albion centre-forward, although never looking the same powerhouse that he had been when topping the Division One scoring charts the season before, was still scoring consistently — and Tony Brown was not far behind, scoring his fifth of the season in a 6-2 hammering at Highbury.

The Albion striking pair were rewarded for their fine form when they were both called into the Football League squad for a representative match against the Irish League at Carrow Road on September 23. The *Albion News* proudly recorded their selection: "Congratulations to our hot-shots, Jeff Astle and Tony Brown, who were drafted into the Football League squad to meet the Irish League at Norwich in mid-week. It was quite an honour for the popular Hawthorns duo to be called on by Sir Alf Ramsey."

A pointer to the future, perhaps, for Tony Brown, for at this point the management of the Football League representative sides had been transferred from the League Committee to the national team manager, and the games, although declining in popularity and importance, now formed a logical step-up in the ladder to full international recognition.

Astle, of course, was already in possession of his England caps, although he was very much a fringe player in the winger-free Ramsey England sides of the time, and he started the game at Norwich, and scored two goals; Brown was nominated as a substitute, but came on for Ian Storey Moore in the second half and scored as well, so the Albion contingent gave full value for their selection.

The game, in the event, proved to be Astle's swan song at international level, for he never represented his country again at any level. His goals dried up abruptly, and he netted on just six occasions in the final 31 games of the season. Fortunately for the Albion, who had relied on Astle's goal power to maintain their place in Division One for the past six seasons, his decline was matched by the inexorable rise and rise of Bomber Brown, who soon took over the mantle of Albion's goalscorer supreme — a title he was to hold, in the main, for the next eight years!

Steadily, the goals began to flow for Brown in that autumn of 1970, but he really game to prominence with a superb hat-trick against Tottenham at The Hawthorns on December 12. Martin Chivers gave the Londoners the lead after 25 minutes, but in the second half, attacking the favoured Birmingham Road, the Bomber took command. In the 48th minute, he equalised, being on hand to fire the ball past pat Jennings after the Northern Ireland international goalkeeper had pushed out Suggett's initial effort.

In the 77th minute, Albion took the lead from the penalty spot, Brown netting from twelve yards with his usual power and accuracy after Beal had brought down Suggett in the area, and four minutes after that, Brown completed his hat-trick. As the *Express & Star* reported: "Don't say Brown — say goals! Astle seized on a loose ball, squared a pass across goal and Brown thumped home a devastating right footer"

As if in challenge to the hubris of the Albion chairman, who had dismissed the hard-earned cup success of the previous six years, Albion's flirtation with the knock-out competitions ended with a sickening thud. In the League Cup, Tottenham's 5-0 whitewash at White Hart Lane was the Albion's worst ever defeat in the competition. In the new "British Isles Cup", Albion lost home and away to lowly Greenock Morton, who were hardly setting the League alight in Scotland, whilst in the FA Cup, things were little better.

There was a terrible struggle to oust minnows Scunthorpe United in the Third Round as the Ironsides — Kevin Keegan and all — were rather unlucky not to win the first encounter at The Hawthorns. It took two opportunistic goals from Brown in the Old Show Ground replay to see Albion through.

In the fourth round, luck deserted the Albion once more, just as it had at Hillsborough the year before. At home to Ipswich Town — who Albion had eliminated from the League Cup on their way to Wembley in 1969 — Colin Suggett gave Albion the lead. With four minutes left on the clock, Brown raced away clear of the Ipswich defence and rounded goalkeeper Laurie Sivell to fire what would have surely been the clinching goal into the net. It never reached it — Mick Mills, racing back to cover, managed to get to the goal line in time to palm the ball onto the bar!

Brown was stunned. "It should have definitely been a penalty. An Ipswich defender came around the back of me and palmed the ball so that it rose and hit the bar. Otherwise, I must have scored. I appealed for hands, but the referee seemed to be of the opinion that the ball had struck the defender's head!"

The iniquity of the decision was rubbed in when the Suffolk side scored a shock equaliser in the second minute of injury time — and Albion lost the replay, miserably, at Portman Road, in what was probably Brown's poorest game of the season. The reason? His old colleague Ian Collard. As the *Express & Star* picked out — "Collard was designated the task of man-marking Tony Brown. He did his job ruthlessly, shadowing the Albion top scorer into almost complete ineffectiveness"

The shackling of the Bomber was not the only reason for Albion's 3-0 defeat — the cup tie was merely a reflection of a trend that had been obvious all season. For all their attacking flair and goal power at The Hawthorns, this Albion side were incapable of turning it one away from home. True, Brown or, in the past, Astle, might grab their side a goal, but the shaky and ageing defence, and the midfield, which relied so heavily on the slowing legs of Scot

Bobby Hope, were incapable of holding any sort of lead away from the support of their own fans in West Bromwich.

As the League season came to its close, Albion had not won away for an incredible fourteen months, the worst such run in the club's history, and it looked certain that, for the first time since 1891-92, the club would go through an entire campaign without collecting the full two points in any away game.

At the end of January, Ashman had called in the players for crisis talks following another unedifying 4-1 defeat in front of the *Match of The Day* cameras at Chelsea — he realised that it only needed the team to lose its Fortress Hawthorns touch, and they would soon be staring relegation in the face. "I can remember it well when Alan called us all into the dressing room. He was very upset — almost in tears — about the way things were going with the team. It was the usual sort of crisis talk from a manager, about how we were letting ourselves and the fans down, that sort of thing, but it seemed to do the job."

Tony (centre) with Derek Parkin and Ralph Coates with England in Malta

Whatever the gist of the meeting, it seemed to have the desired effect — almost! In their very next away game, once more back in London, Albion took on Spurs at White Hart Lane, scene of their 5-0 humiliation in the League Cup, and seemingly a perfect test for the new, Ashman-stiffened defensive resolve, as the Londoners were a lovely, free-scoring side, particularly at home. Albion raced into a fourth minute lead; and it was a particularly significant goal for Tony Brown, who raced onto a defence splitting pass from Asa Hartford to drill his hundredth League goal — scored a full year "ahead of schedule" — past the advancing Pat Jennings. Then came the test. Alan Mullery equalised in the 26th minute from a penalty, then shot wide from a second spot kick twenty minutes later. Brown popped up with goal 101 to give the Albion the lead once more, and it looked as if the side were home and dry with that first away win under their belt. Then, deep in injury time, with Jim Cumbes limping badly in the Albion goal, a Gilzean header powered against the crossbar and bounced down onto the line. The Albion defenders claimed that the ball had not crossed the line; the referee thought otherwise; Albion's hopes were thwarted and Spurs were level, with the whistle for full time blowing almost immediately afterwards.

Despite the problems away from home, Tony, at any rate, was enjoying a real purple patch in his career. During February and March 1971, he scored no less than eleven of his side's fourteen goals — including a hat-trick the annual goal-fest against Manchester United.

George Best opened the scoring for United in the 18th minute, but fourteen minutes later Brown levelled when Stepney dropped a Kaye free kick and the Bomber made no mistake with a right foot blast. Within 35 seconds of the start of the second half, Brown was on target again.

The match programme for Tony's game for the League side at Hampden Park

Hartford fed McVitie for a shot which was blocked in the area, and once again Brown was there to pick up the pieces.

Back came United to level once more through Aston, but in the 55th minute Brown crowned a magnificent performance when he tore after a huge clearance from Jim Cumbes. He held off a challenge from Dunne before connecting with another right foot shot which easily beat the stranded Stepney to complete his second hat-trick of the season — and reach 24 goals by the first week in March. Still United came back, and in the end, Albion won the game 4-3 only thanks to a last minute header from John Wile.

The First Division's top scorer made more progress on the international front, with a call-up to Alf Ramsey's England squad for their European Championship qualifying match against Malta in Valletta. The problem was — locating Tony to let him know he was required to travel to the Mediterranean island! He was away in Manchester, visiting his family on the weekend of the announcement, and could not be easily contacted. Alan Ashman received a call from the Football Association in the evening then had to contact an Albion scout in Manchester to ask him to get in touch with the player. The scout got hold of Tony's grandmother, who gave him the telephone number of the next door neighbour of his mother's, who popped round to give Tony the good news!

After all that, Tony failed to get a game. He was named as one of the substitutes, as England scraped through 1-0, but the honour of the call-up was enough for Tony. "I was in the England parties a few times under Alf Ramsey. They were great squads in those days, and if you even broke into the squad, it was a great honour."

The Football League side at Hampden. Back row (l-r): Todd, Hollins, Parkin, Jackson, McFarland, Moore. Front row: Coates, O'Neill, Reaney, Tony Brown, Hurst, Storey-Moore

Further reward for Tony's goal-scoring exploits came on March 17 when he played for the Scottish League side against the pick of the Scottish League at Hampden Park. "Playing at Hampden Park was really something — it had a great atmosphere. I think that any selection for the Football League was a great thing; it was an extension to your normal club career, and I loved those games." Even better was the win, as England came away with a 1-0 victory thanks to a goal from Ralph Coates.

Back in the League, time was running out for Albion to pick up that elusive away win. Another near miss came at the home of the First Division Champions, Everton, where Albion raced into a 2-0 lead after just eight minutes, thanks to goals from Brown and Astle — but were 3-2 down after less than half an hour! In the end, a 78th minute equaliser from John Wile came as an unexpected bonus in a match that really should have been won by the Baggies.

With just six away games left, there were some terrible trips in store, including games at Anfield and — most feared of all — Elland Road, where the classy Leeds United side had not been beaten, in League, Cup or in European competition, for nearly two years; their home record was as good as Albion's away record was bad!

It looked as if Albion's best bet for that away win was at Upton Park, where Albion had grabbed a couple of good wins in the past three years, and when Astle gave them an early lead, a good result did look on the cards. Yet once more, the defence crumbled, conceded a soft equaliser and lost to an 86th minute goal from a striker who had always scored profusely against the Albion, Jimmy Greaves.

The trip to Anfield proved to be less harrowing than expected. Tony Brown scored in front of the Kop for the third time in four years, with a goal of added significance — it was his 28th of the season in all competitions, surpassing his previous best return of 27 (which included ten goals in the League Cup) in 1965-66. It also looked as if it might also be the goal to break the club's away hoodoo, until Alun Evans popped up with an 83rd minute equaliser to maintain the Reds' excellent home record.

Tony scores the opening — and quite legitimate — goal at Leeds

When that long-awaited away win did at last arise, on the back of the most efficient, controlled away performance of the season, it caused enormous controversy, the repercussions of which were to reverberate in the game for many seasons, as the winning goal stopped the match, lost a Championship — according to Don Revie and Johnny Giles, at least — and provoked a ground "riot" that was seen all over the country thanks to the *Match of the Day* cameras and the over the top hysteria of commentator Barry Davies.

Yes — Albion, with typical perversity, chose Elland Road to put in their best exhibition of football of the season. Before the game, the match had been featured on the BBC's *Football Focus*, when Leeds' Irish international midfield genius Johnny Giles had given an interview which implied that the visit of the Albion was an opportunity for his great Leeds side to improve their goal average in their epic battle with Arsenal for the First Division Championship. "Yes, we saw Football Focus during the pre-match meal at our hotel, and that riled us — a few of the players were a bit upset at the way Gilesy made out we were going to get slaughtered."

Albion arrived in Yorkshire four places off the bottom of the table, to all intents and purposes safe enough from relegation with a seven point gap between them and the bottom two, with just four games left to play. Leeds United, on the other hand, had everything to play for at the top of the table. Having played 38 games, they had garnered 58 points (almost double Albion's total from the same number of games) and had only lost four League games all season — and none at Elland Road.

Ugly scenes at Elland Road sparked off by Albion's second goal

Two points behind, but with two games in hand, and a visit to Leeds to come, lay Bertie Mee's Arsenal, who were deeply involved in the FA Cup and were facing the sort of fixture congestion usually associated with Don Revie's customary trawl for trophies. Goal average considerations were an obvious concern for Leeds, especially as they had beaten Albion 4-0, 5-1 and 5-0 on the ground in recent seasons — but for once, Albion were no lambs to the slaughter!

And at the centre of the controversy that was about to erupt was one Tony Brown. In the 18th minute he shocked the Leeds faithful with a splendidly taken goal. A terrible pass from Jack Charlton gave Astle a chance to send Colin Suggett down the right. Brown ran intelligently into the open space for the return pass and had plenty of time to pick his spot and shoot past Sprake as the Welsh international goalkeeper came off his line.

There is no question that Leeds were not playing at their fluent best, but much of that was down to the excellent harrying and forcing by the Albion midfield and defence, in which recent signing John Wile was a tower of strength. The home crowd, brought up on a solid diet of Leeds wins, got more and more frustrated, both at the inadequacy of their own side and at Albion's new, and thoroughly effective offside trap, which repeatedly caught Allan Clarke, Peter Lorimer and Mick Jones in its jaws, the latter having a "goal" disallowed for offside shortly after the interval.

If the atmosphere on the terraces was getting ugly, as the notoriously partisan home supporters got more and more frustrated, it was nothing to what exploded in the 68th minute, when the Albion had the temerity to score a second and ultimately decisive goal, laid on a plate for Jeff Astle by Tony Brown.

In the 69th minute a Leeds attack was broken down in midfield when Tony stuck out a leg to stop a wayward pass from Norman Hunter. He failed to gain immediate control as the ball bounced at speed off his leg, and with Colin Suggett still ambling back in the middle of the pitch from a previous Albion attack, the two Leeds defenders furthest back, Hunter and Reaney, both raised their hands in a confident appeal for offside against the former Sunderland man — confident enough, at least, to stop Tony in his tracks.

To their horror, even though the linesman on the opposite side of the field had raised his flag, referee Ray Tinkler waved play on. An astonished Brown took a second or two to compose himself before continuing his run down the right, with only Sprake in between him and the goal. Instead of trying his luck with a shot, Brown delayed his pass until strike partner Jeff Astle came in with a supporting run, and with perfect timing Brown slipped the ball across the box for Astle to sidefoot almost apologetically into the net.

Astle turned away to commence his usual goal celebrations — until he took a look at just how ugly the crowd had turned, and soon ran for safety in the centre circle. Except that this time, even that was no haven, as Leeds fans stormed onto the pitch to get at, in particular, the referee. Dozens of police followed to try to protect the referee and the Albion players, and there were several violent scuffles between the two factions, with several people taken to hospital. Meanwhile, poor innocent linesman Mr Cartlich, an unfortunate late replacement for the game, was struck on the head by a bottle and had to receive lengthy treatment from the Leeds trainer.

After a lengthy break, with fans still fighting on the terraces, the game was restarted — following a warning that the game would be abandoned if there was any more trouble — with a long line of police positioned along the touchline, facing towards the angry popular side of the ground, later to be pelted with cans and cushions when Mr Tinkler compounded his perceived felonies by turning down the desperate appeals from the home players for a penalty against John Wile.

Three minutes from time, under great provocation, Albion conceded their usual soft goal, but this time they held out for that longed for win —and were able to enjoy the re-run on *Match of The Day* five hours later. Tinkler explained his decision; "The man who took the ball

Goal number thirty of a fantastic season goes past Bob Wilson to earn a 2-2 draw

through [Brown] was not offside. Suggett was in an offside position but he was not interfering with play. I was not frightened. I just wanted to get on with the game. I think the police did a very good job."

Don Revie, the Leeds manager, was beside himself with rage. "It was a disgraceful decision. We have taken it fairly and squarely like gentlemen but when you get beaten by a decision like that it is unbelievable. Suggett was five yards offside. When the game was held up I spoke to one of the linesmen, Mr Troupe, and he said 'He was offside Mr Revie'." Typically, Revie blamed the crowd scenes on the referee. "We have the most placid crowd in the world(!) but he could have had a riot. There were not enough people on the pitch to cause the match to be abandoned."

Revie's anger, fuelled by the fact that Arsenal had beaten Newcastle 1-0 to topple Leeds off their perch, was outrageously supported by Barry Davies of the BBC, as everybody seemed to miss the point that Suggett was, indeed, not interfering with play, despite being in an offside position, and that had Leeds played to the whistle, the goal might well have been prevented. Never once was it mentioned on the programme that the Albion had been the better side throughout, and had thoroughly deserved to win. Tony thought Tinkler was right. "Suggett was definitely interfering with play, and I was in my own half when I intercepted the ball. If anything, I think that Jeff might have been offside when I made the final pass for the goal, but you can't tell from the camera angle on the video."

The Football Association's view was very different. After Leeds had been pipped at the post for the 1971 Championship by the Arsenal, who won the Double after beating Liverpool at Wembley, they received the bad news that Elland Road was to be closed for the opening games of the following season in punishment for the disgraceful scenes at the Albion game — a decision which some Leeds supporters still claim cost them the Championship in 1972 as well! Certainly the bad feeling between the supporters of the two clubs was still evident eleven years when Leeds fans ran riot at The Hawthorns after Ronnie Allen's Albion side relegated their team in a crucial end of season clash.

Irony of ironies, Albion's next game seven days later was at home — to Arsenal! In the eyes of Leeds supporters, they rubbed salt in the gaping wound they had already caused by handing Arsenal an own goal and struggling to a 2-2 draw against the future Champions. Tony Brown, of course, was in the thick of the action once more, scoring an 86th minute leveller against the Gunners — his 30th goal of a momentous season.

But the best was still to come. Before the game, Brown had collected the trophy for the *Midland Footballer of The Year* from the Albion

Tony Brown at Wembley, standing proudly in his England shirt, before his full international debut against Wales in 1971

chairman, but the supreme accolade for any professional footballer — the full international cap — was only just around the corner. On Wednesday May 19, Tony returned to Wembley to pull on the white shirt of England in the Home International fixture against Wales. "When I reported for training with England, I had no great hopes of being selected. I considered it an achievement even to be included in the Home International party. Then, after training, Sir Alf announced his team and my name was included, it was fabulous news. It took some time to sink in. He later congratulated me and then I realised that my big break had arrived!"

"Sir Alf was a great organiser. I remember whenever I went for training with England sides, how meticulous Alf was, in everything he did. Free kicks, for and against, corners, throw-ins; everything was organised spot on, so you always knew what you had to do in every situation. Such attention to detail. Before the game, he said to me 'You've got in the England side because of what you've done at your club. Just go out and do the same' — but, of course, I couldn't, because I'd been given a different role, and it was a nightmare for me."

The game was a giant anti-climax for Brown. In a sterile game (described as "England's most ineffective since winning the World Cup in 1966") the sides drew 0-0, Tony heading over Gary Sprake's bar with virtually his first touch as an international player — a rare clear chance in an awful match. When England did net in the second half, through Francis Lee, it was unfortunate that Tony was standing in an offside position, and the goal was disallowed. Soon after, Tony was taken off and replaced by Leeds' Allan Clarke, and that was the end of his brush with international football.

As Tony says now, in retrospect, "The international I played was not a great success, but I got my cap and I can say that I played for my country — they can't take that away from me. I wasn't asked to play for England the same way I played for my club — it was more like the way Don Howe wanted me to play later in my career, as an out and out striker, and that wasn't my style and it didn't really work."

Ramsey wanted Brown to play with his back to goal, almost in a Geoff Hurst-type role, rather than in the style that had brought him so many goals that season for his club, as a midfielder bursting through with the ball always in front of him, feeding off a target man. As a result, both player and country lost out, and Tony had to be content to continue his career in the Football League — as the most prolific goalscorer the club has ever had; more than enough recompense, as far as Albion supporters are concerned, for an international career stopped in the bud!

Don Howe returns home...

In the summer of 1971, Jim Gaunt and the rest of the Albion board decided to act on their demands for League success. The previous season had ended dismally, with the side slipping down as low as 17th in Division One — as low as they had been since a similar finish in 1955 — whilst in London, a former Albion star, Don Howe, had made a significant contribution in coaching Arsenal to a League and Cup Double — with a little help from the Baggies!

Whatever the merits of sacking one of only three team managers to have taken the club to a major trophy (a record he unfortunately still holds to this day), it was the manner of Alan Ashman's dismissal that was so disgraceful. The likeable Ashman — who certainly had the full support of his playing staff, if not the board — only learned about his sacking from a waiter at his hotel on holiday in Greece, and had to get the local newspapers translated to discover that Don Howe had been given his first managerial post in his stead.

For all their private support of Ashman, the players were powerless to do anything about it. "The lads were very upset because we'd had some good times under Alan, but there's nothing that you can do as

Dark days ahead for Tony, and the Albion, should they but know it. Don Howe arrives as manager in 1971 (with Bobby Hope, John Wile and Graham Lovett)

players, because the directors make the decisions. I always thought that there were certain similarities between Alan Ashman and Jimmy Hagan, despite the differences in personality — both were good managers, and both won a trophy for the club."

Always sadly underrated, Alan Ashman went on to manage in Greece, with Olympiakos, before returning triumphantly to take former club Carlisle United into their only spell in the top flight in 1974-75, winding down his full-time career as manager at Walsall and assistant manager at Derby County and Hereford United.

His replacement, Don Howe was one of Albion's favourite sons. A quality full-back who had been capped 23 times for England, he served Albion for nearly ten years before leaving, somewhat acrimoniously, in 1964, after several disputes with manager Jimmy Hagan (including the infamous "tracksuit saga"), to join Arsenal for a substantial £45,000 fee. His playing career was soon terminated by a broken leg which forced him to move into coaching somewhat earlier than anticipated, but his influence on the Gunners' brand of methodical but winning football was widely acknowledged alongside the inexperienced Bertie Mee.

Several of his one-time Albion playing colleagues were still at The Hawthorns, and players such as John Kaye, Bobby Hope and, of course, Tony Brown were wondering how Howe's tactics and methodology would affect them at the Albion — a club for many years noted for flair and exciting attacking football.

"After Alan left, Don Howe arrived. It was a shock at the time, because he'd just won the Double with Arsenal, and it was a big surprise that the Albion managed to get him, but he obviously had a feeling for the Albion after being here for so long. I think he was actually captain on the day that I had made my debut at Ipswich back in 1963 — a tremendous player, one of the first attacking full-backs.

At the first meeting upstairs at Spring Road, Don introduced himself, along with George Wright and Brian Whitehouse. He told us he was going to make us League Champions, win the Cup and make the blue and white stripes as famous as Real Madrid all-white kit. He came with great ideas, but, personally speaking, at least, it was a rough time. Training was harder, more demanding and time-consuming, with more emphasis on fitness, which came as quite a shock, and more concentration on working defensively as a unit."

Some of Howe's training methods did not go down well. "He brought this long rope to training one morning, and tied it round three midfielder players — me, Len Cantello and Asa Hartford, and then he'd throw the ball to one side and I'd have to run after it. And, of course, I'd pull Len, and he'd pull Asa and we'd all be dragged over to that side of the pitch. Then he'd throw it to the other side, and Asa would have to chase after it, and so on. It was to show us how to keep together on the pitch, but he had to do it with this bloody rope. We were all experienced players, and he should have just explained it to us. It looked bloody hilarious, and all the other lads were on the side, and Jeff in particular, laughing their heads off!"

Yet for Tony, it was back to "business as usual" as the '71-72 season opened with an away tie in the novel sponsored Watney Cup competition. It was ironic that Don Howe, whose Albion side would soon come to be recognised for their dourness and lack of goals, would commence his appointment in an invitation tournament that was seen as a reward for attacking football!

Tony scored twice in the quarter-final tie at the Racecourse Ground, Wrexham, taking advantage of the experimental change to the offside rules that meant that players could only be offside in the last eighteen yards of the pitch. Ominously, though, the *News of The World* reported that after the game, the Welshmen were complaining about the rough treatment they had received from the Albion defenders.

The following Wednesday, there was another trip to unfamiliar locations as the club paid its first ever visit to The Shay — and beat Halifax Town, conquerors of Manchester United four days previously. Albion did not make the same mistake, but once again, exerted a formidable physical presence, with bookings for John Kaye, Lyndon Hughes and Asa Hartford.

On Saturday August 7, Albion had home advantage in the Watney Cup Final against Fourth Division Colchester United, still basking in the fame they had won in their shock win against Leeds United in the FA Cup the season before. Captaining United was a man to whom The Hawthorns was a very familiar venue — Tony's former colleague, and predecessor as "penalty king", Bobby Cram. Penalties were to be very significant that day, for after a thrilling 4-4 draw, after extra time, five players stepped up from each side to settle the destination of the cup in Albion's first-ever penalty shoot-out.

Surprisingly, Bobby Cram missed his spot-kick — but Tony, and Jeff Astle, were both successful, although both had to retake their kicks after goalkeeper Graham Smith was adjudged to have moved too early before saving both of them. Unfortunately, both Ray Wilson and Len Cantello missed their kicks and Colchester inflicted Don Howe's first defeat in his new job. It was something he — and Tony Brown — were to get used to in the next four seasons.

The side knuckled down to the bread and butter of the League. In the first game, against West Ham, at Upton Park, Albion made a mockery of the "soft touch away from home" label which they picked up in previous years, upsetting the home crowd with some tigerish tackling — and a 38th minute goal from Bomber Brown.

Tony netted in the next two unbeaten games as well, at home to Everton (2-0) and Coventry (1-1) and, as usual against the Red Devils, in the fourth, away to Manchester United. Away — but not at Old Trafford, which had, like Elland Road, been closed for the opening games because of crowd trouble. Instead, the game was played in midweek at Stoke's Victoria Ground, with the winners guaranteed top place in the First Division. It was a match too far for Don Howe's battlers. With George Best in brilliant form, Albion were soon three goals down, and Tony's last minute consolation goal was an irrelevance.

The Baggies bounced back and travelled to new leaders Sheffield United. Missing Jeff Astle, Howe went for midfield hard man to wear the number nine shirt, with Tony left to plough a lonely furrow up front. As for the defence... for a team normally known for free flowing football, the Sunday papers made interesting reading. The *Sunday Express* declared "Albion will win no friends at all with this fumbling brand of negative football — they had more destroyers that the Russian fleet". The Sun proclaimed "During ninety frustrating, futile minutes Howe's heavies leaned on United to the full". In the first half alone, the Albion committed sixteen fouls and had Ray Wilson and — shock horror — Bobby Hope booked!

With such tactics, it was no surprise that Albion lost six out of their next seven games (including a first ever home defeat in the League Cup), scoring just one goal. Naturally, that was from Tony, scoring from the rebound after Ipswich's Laurie Sivell had pushed his penalty kick onto the crossbar.

In that same game, Tony had a new strike partner. With Astle suffering from poor form and injury problems, Howe had made his first foray into the transfer market with the signing of ex-Gunner Bobby Gould, from neighbours Wolves, for a fee of £60,000. Quite apart from the fact that nobody could replace "The King" in the eyes of the Birmingham Road end, it was hard to see how the bustling style of Gould would fit in alongside the stealth of the Bomber. "I think Don brought in Gouldy to bring that sort of bustling enthusiasm into the team, and because he knew him from Arsenal, and he was somebody he could trust — and he scored a few goals."

There was one useful result, a 2-0 win at Crystal Palace, when Astle, Brown and Gould lined up together for the first time, but thereafter Albion's form slumped from bad to worse. Amidst rumours of unrest at the club, with criticism of training methods and tactics, Brown's goals dried up, along with Astle's — but in all fairness, it was Albion's style of play that meant that goal chances were few and far between. Add to that Gould's struggle to settle into the side, and the barracking that the future Albion manager was receiving from a disgruntled Hawthorns crowd brought up on the silkier skills of the likes of Allen and Astle at centre-forward, and it clear that the side was in deep, deep trouble. It was no wonder that by the time that Albion lost 3-0 at Elland Road — and how that pleased the home crowd — they slipped into bottom place in the First Division.

And that was not the end of it. Between November 6 and December 18, Albion lost seven games on the trot, conceding 19 goals and scoring only six, including a humiliating trip for Howe back to Highbury, when Arsenal completed another "Double" — at home and away over the Albion in the League!

By the time Liverpool visited The Hawthorns on December 27, Albion were rock bottom with just eleven points from 22 games, and with only three wins to their name. In his programme notes for the match, Howe was sanguine. "Despite the fact that results have been going against us, I have received whole-hearted support from the players both in training and on the field. Our disappointing situation cannot be blamed on lack of effort!"

Tony recalls a big crisis meeting at the time. "Jim Gaunt, the chairman at the time, had all of us in the old boardroom, which was only the second time I'd ever been in there, since they'd shown be round the club in 1961, to convince me to sign. Gaunt said 'You don't look as if you're enjoying your football any more; everybody looks miserable. Get out and start enjoying yourselves. Take no notice of what HE says' — pointing at Don Howe — 'Just get out there and enjoy it'. I couldn't believe he'd said that about Don in front of us all!"

The Baggies lined up against the Reds with recent signing Graham Smith — the same goalkeeper who had won the Watney Cup for Colchester in August — in goal, and Bobby Gould up front for Astle. Two old stagers were missing; John Kaye had been sold to Hull City and, even more unthinkable, former essential playmaker Bobby Hope had been dropped into the Reserves.

As the latecomers filed into the ground to swell the crowd of 43,000, some would have missed the shock fifth minute goal scored by the Bomber — the goal that was to turn the season around, and maintain Albion's place in the top flight for another season, at least. A big boot from new captain John Wile was misheaded by stand-in centre-half Ian Ross and Tony was there to lift the ball over a stranded Clemence and into the net off the post.

For the rest of the game, it was a real backs-to-the-wall battle, in which the Smith had his only really good game for the club, as the Baggies held out for a belated Christmas present of two points. Could Albion maintain their recovery in the difficult game at Ipswich the following week? Howe fielded the same side, but hopes of any continuation of the revival seemed to have been ended by two goals for the home side — managed by Howe's former Albion playing colleague, Bobby Robson — in the first fifty minutes

On the hour Bomber started the fight-back when he smashed home a pass from Gould, who scored an equaliser twelve minutes later. Eight minutes from the end, George McVitie broke away to score a shock winner to cap one of the best recoveries by any Albion side in the last thirty years — and the only way was up, from then on.

Two more goals from Tony against Sheffield United in a 2-2 draw hauled Albion off the bottom of the table, and although the side dipped out of the FA Cup at home to Coventry soon after — and Tony was denied a goal by a blatant punch off the line by City defender Bobby Parker — form improved so much that relegation was soon a forgotten problem. Indeed, by the time League leaders Manchester United came to The Hawthorns at the end of January, a recalled Jeff Astle was able to round off a confident Albion performance with a classic headed winner.

Tony's kept up his scoring with a superb winning volley past Peter Shilton at Filbert Street, and another decider in a 3-2 home win over Southampton, and by the beginning of April, Albion had all but secured First Division safety, with only three defeats since that crucial win against Liverpool. On April 8, Tony was injured and missed his first game of the season at home to Tottenham. As luck would have it, the side were awarded a penalty — and the Smethwick End net bulged, for once, with a penalty kick from somebody other than Tony Brown, as Bobby Hope stepped to score from the spot.

Tony was back the following week, though, for the match that would officially confirm Albion's escape from the drop — and there was no better place to celebrate than Molineux! It took just fifty five seconds for Tony to get the all important goal after Phil Parkes had saved a cross-shot from Alistair Brown, as he bundled the ball over the line in the front of the North Bank, and Albion ended a traumatic season in 16th place — a one position improvement over the previous campaign.

Brown finished the season with 17 goals. In its way, that tally was just as remarkable as the thirty goals he had scored the previous season, when it is considered that they were scored for a struggling, dour defensive side that had looked dead and buried by Christmas. It was a wonder he was scoring at all, as Howe had begun to tamper with the very way he played his game — very much the way Sir Alf Ramsey had tried to do in his England appearance.

"Don tried to change my whole style of playing. I had a meeting with him and he told me he was going to make me a better all-round player, with my back to goal instead of coming through. But I wasn't cut out to play that way; I had to be looking the way I was playing, feeding off a big man. I could never play with my back to goal, holding it, shielding it, but he tried to make me play that way. But I couldn't do it — I felt uncomfortable doing it. He also called me in and told me that as I was coming to the end of my career, I needed to do extra training, on my own. And I was only 27, and had just scored thirty goals in a season. I found that really alarming! As a result, I lost a lot of confidence, and lost form — bad days, they were."

At the end of that first season in the job, Howe admitted that he had done things wrong, especially regarding Brown. "I must confess we messed Tony Brown about a bit before we found the right way to use him. We had been told that one of his strengths was coming from behind, but we discovered that in midfield, defensive duties held him back. By allowing Tony to go forward I felt he would be sure to get goals. I would add that although Tony has not scored so many goals as last season, he has had just as many chances but they have not gone in for him so well."

So, after deciding that Tony's style of play was all wrong — despite having scored 30 goals — Howe tried to change his style of play; then relied on the "new" striker to score the goals which saved the club from relegation. Howe, unfortunately, would not be so lucky a second time.

The 1972-73 season began with friendlies at Feyenoord and Hibernian and a short three match tour of Sweden. As the season commenced, Brown could reflect on almost ten years at the club, all of them spent in the top flight. He had played over 300 League games for the club, but his enthusiasm for the game — and for the club itself — were undiminished. He had put on his shooting boots once more, opening his account with a goal in Sweden against Landskroner, and was looking forward to another season amongst the hot-shots of the First Division.

How quickly it all went wrong. Albion got off to a terrible start, failing to win any of their first seven League games — and Tony endured the worst starts to his own personal scoring campaign. By the seventh match, at Everton, he had failed to get on the scoresheet even once, and had been relegated to the substitute's bench. Indeed, it took a penalty to get him started for the domestic season, as Albion struggled with the help of a spot kick and an own goal, to beat Second Division Queens Park Rangers in the League Cup.

Three days later, Tony gave Albion their first League win of the season against First Division Champions Derby County at The Hawthorns with a right foot shot in the 67th minute, after Bobby Gould had equalised an early Roy McFarland goal. Those goals heralded the start of a six match unbeaten run which ended with a defeat at Maine Road on September 30, which also marked Tony's first away goal of the season, on "home territory" for him. It was one of his best. The local press recorded it. "Albion, who were much worse than City in a generally poor game, levelled the score in the 58th minute with a fine goal by Tony Brown. The Albion striker set off on a long run deep into the City half of the field, with two defenders in pursuit. He took them on and finished brilliantly by slotting the ball low into the corner of the net."

The next League game, back at The Hawthorns, was also against a Manchester side, as Albion took on struggling United in what was always the highlight of the Albion's season. They certainly got off to a bright enough start, two goals up from Ally Brown in the first twenty minutes, only for George Best to pull a goal back from the spot. Then it was Tony's turn. A minute before the break, Asa Hartford was tripped by Ian Donald in the area. With the crowd shouting for Ally Brown to take the kick, to complete his hat-trick, Tony was in the unusual position of taking a penalty against the fans' wishes. Sod's law dictated that he would miss —and he did. For once, he ignored his usual inclination to blast the ball, and tried to place it to Stepney's right, and only succeeded in stroking the ball past the post. Ian Moore scored a second half equaliser for United and a valuable point was lost, particularly as United were to be one of Albion's rivals in another relegation struggle after Christmas.

The miss, of course, did not lessen Tony's enthusiasm for taking penalties, and the following week it was back to normal as he hammered another against Chelsea at Stamford Bridge in a 3-1 defeat. It was a good spell for Tony. Two more goals followed against Newcastle in the Texaco Cup, another — watched by Sir Alf Ramsey — in a 1-1 draw against Spurs at White Hart Lane and two more in a 2-1 win over fellow strugglers Stoke City.

By Christmas, lack of consistency saw Albion — as the previous year — in the relegation zone, with just five League wins from 22 games although Tony had shaken off his poor start to record a respectable twelve goals from 27 League and cup games.

Yet in November the West Bromwich Albion stalwart had so nearly left the club! "I never ASKED to move away from the Albion, but I nearly went in the end. I nearly went to Selhurst Park. Crystal Palace had Bert Head as manager and a new wealthy chairman came in, and they bought Charlie Cooke and Don Rogers, and wanted to sign me as well. I spoke to Bert Head and we fixed up a few things. Don wanted me to go, but for some reason a block was put on the move from the Albion end, and I never went. Personally, I didn't want to go, but we had a chat, finalised things, and a fee was fixed at £175,000, which was a lot of money then. I think the Albion directors put a stop to it."

Had Brown gone to Selhurst Park, it would have culminated a remarkable clear-out by Howe, who seemed determined to sell all his experienced players — the men who had done so well under Hagan and Ashman — and replace them with talented but vastly inexperienced youngsters from the Reserves.

"We lost John Kaye, Bobby Hope, Jeff Astle — a lot of experienced players went, as he got rid of all of them — except me! Jeff was having his four cartilages out and he was struggling and Don got rid of him, but getting rid of Bobby Hope to Blues was a surprise, as he was after him when he was at Arsenal! Colin Suggett went to Norwich, after converting him to a midfielder, and then he tried to get me out as well. He changed it all round too suddenly, so there were too many youngsters in at one time. Youngsters can't cope with it by themselves.".

In December 1972 Tony was joined in the Albion side by fiery Scottish international Willie Johnston, a £135,000 signing from Glasgow Rangers. "I think that signing Willie was the best thing Don ever did for the club. He was tremendous to play with, very professional, despite his sendings-off. Teams had to put two men on him, which was great for me, playing on his side of the pitch, because it gave me so much room on the inside."

At the same time, just as Howe brought in a man to provide a big forward with the ammunition from the wings to score the goals that were so sorely lacking — he sold centre-forward Bobby Gould to Bristol City, leaving the side without a recognised leader in attack, as Jeff Astle, still on the injured list, had not started a game all season. "All the players thought Don was unapproachable. He wouldn't listen to anybody, and after getting rid of the experienced players, brought in too many youngsters who just didn't have the right amount of experience. He took Ally Robertson out, and brought in Dave Rushbury. When things are going wrong, you need your Robbos, because he was a winner, who always gave everything."

There were some good youngsters coming through, of course. "Alan Merrick was a REAL hard man. I've seen him sort Giles and Bremner out with one tackle, when we played against Leeds. He put both of them on their backsides and never batted an eyelid! A bit one-paced, but as a full-back he could get away with it, by positional play. You didn't want to be in a tackle with Alan, because there was only going to be one winner, but he'd go through a brick wall for the Albion; a good lad, and Albion through and through, like a few other defenders who came through at that time, like Gordon Nisbet and Roger Minton — but you can't beat experience."

After the Christmas programme, curtailed by the weather which caused the postponement of the home game with Leeds United, Howe, as he had done at the same time the previous year, took his side for a mid-winter break to Jersey. This time, however, there was to be no miracle cure.

On January 9 1973 the Bomber played in his 400th first class game for the Albion at Bramall Lane, but there was no celebrating as Sheffield United won easily. An FA Cup four match epic against Nottingham Forest provided some distraction from League troubles, but the cup run came to an end at Elland Road, and it was time "to concentrate on the League" — and by the time of that FA Cup exit, Albion were propping up the table, three points adrift following an amazing 4-0 home defeat by fellow strugglers Crystal Palace.

Brown's form was still good, but the team in general were playing poorly. A dramatic win against Arsenal on February 28 gave them a little hope. It was a significant game for two reasons. It was Albion's first League win at home since beating Ipswich in December — and it renewed Brown's partnership with his favourite strike-partner, Jeff Astle. The "King" had been out of action for ten months, with first cartilage trouble, then appendicitis, but his return inspired Albion and Brown to victory. The *Express and Star*, which had recounted so many Brown-Astle goals in the past, had another to add to the long list. "It was the old Astle-Brown one-two which produced the killer punch in the 57th minute. Willie Johnston crossed from the right, Astle rose at the far post [outjumping a young black debutant by the name of Brendan Batson] and planted a header at Brown's feet which the Bomber dispatched into the corner of the net".

If ever there was a perfect example of the Astle-Brown partnership, this was it. At their peak, the combination had been one of the most successful goal-getting partnerships in the club's history, ahead of names like Glidden and Carter, Bassett and Pearson and Allen and Nicholls. But if the Albion fans thought that the pairing would get them off the hook before the end of the season, they were wrong. The win against Arsenal was another false dawn, as was another surprise win, 4-1 against an Everton side without a goalkeeper for much of the second half. The key match of the entire season — perhaps even of the past quarter of a century, for that was how long Albion had kept their coveted place in the First Division — came on Saturday April 21st, with the visit of Ron Saunders' Norwich City. With three games of the season remaining, for Albion at least, it was clear that two of the bottom three — all on 28 points — were destined for the drop. Norwich were bottom on goal average having played 38 games, with Albion next, having played a game more. Just above them, fifteen hundredths of a goal ahead, from 39 games, were Crystal Palace, with a real tough game at Leeds the same day.

Albion's salvation was in their own hands; a win against Norwich, coupled with the expected defeat for Palace, would probably be enough to keep them up. At half time, the script was going to plan at Elland Road, where Crystal Palace were already three goals down. Less so at The Hawthorns where the game was goal-less although, ominously, Colin Suggett was having a great game in the Norwich midfield. As might be expected from a meeting of two struggling sides managed by Howe and Saunders, the game was not a pretty one, but Albion had enough chances to win it and open upon that vital two point cushion. Instead, four minutes from time, young full-back Roger Minton made a terrible error and gifted a goal to a future Albion team-mate of Brown's, David Cross, who had an easy task of scoring the goal which would sound a death-knell for the Baggies.

Two points adrift of Norwich, that gap increased to a massive four points three days later when the Canaries won their second "crunch" match in a row, with a 2-1 home win over Palace that officially relegated the Londoners. Albion would join them UNLESS they could win both of their last two games, at home to Manchester City on the Wednesday at away to Birmingham City on the Saturday — and then only if Norwich lost at Stoke on the same day.

Amazingly, with two games to win, Howe decided to drop the club's greatest goalscorer for those last two crucial games. Tony was missing from the twelve that went down 2-1 to Manchester City at The Hawthorns on Wednesday April 25 — the game that marked the end of twenty four years of continuous First Division football on the ground — with defender Ally Robertson, in a game that Albion HAD to win, wearing Tony's number seven shirt. On the Saturday, Albion bowed out of the top flight with a fourth consecutive defeat, going down 3-2 to Blues after taking a 2-1 lead through Wile and Astle, and Tony had his final taste of First Division football for three years when he came on as a second half substitute for full-back Minton.

Just five years on from Tony's greatest moment at Wembley in 1968, Albion were falling from grace — and only three players from that wonderful Cup-winning team remained; Astle, Osborne and Brown.

The first of Tony's "great teams" had finally broken up and the Second Division, with the likes of Carlisle, Swindon and Preston, was waiting to ambush the once-proud First Division side. "The feeling that relegation was inevitable had been around for months — throughout the whole club. It was in decline and we could feel that we were going down. I felt it more than most, having been there so long. It was MY club, and it had hurt me to get relegated, more so that players who had been with other clubs straight from school."

Down in the Second Division

Pre-season 1973-74 was a very low key affair compared to previous years — the Albion board needed to tighten their belts after relegation, whilst they could hardly be seen to be rewarding the players for getting relegated by taking them to the other side of the world.

No, it was to lovely Colchester that Tony was sent, as Howe took the unusual step of splitting his squad to play TWO friendlies on the same day. The first choice forward line — including Tony — and the second choice defence went to Layer Road, and the reverse combination travelled to Rhyl. The Welsh non-Leaguers were brushed aside easily enough, but Tony came back, red-faced, after a shambolic team performance that ended 3-0 to the home side.

Games against Wolves, at Molineux, and Bournemouth, at home, followed, and Albion lost them both, without even scoring a goal — the approaching Second Division season was already being viewed with some trepidation. The last time that Albion had played a Second Division match was way back in 1949 when, in the final game of the season, they had lost 1-0 to Grimsby, and missed out on the Championship. It was coincidental that their return to the lower reaches should also be at the seaside.

At Bloomfield Road, in the shadow of Blackpool's famous tower, Tony Brown — who else — opened Albion's account for the season with his first ever goal outside the top flight; and it took him just seven minutes to do it, letting fly with a cross-shot following a pass from David Shaw. Allcock levelled matters for the Seasiders, but further goals from Brown and Glover gave Albion the points before Suddaby scored a last minute consolation.

The following week Albion fans saw the ludicrous sight of knights in shining armour battling it out as part of the pre-match entertainment at The Hawthorns before the game with Crystal Palace, the team that had sunk with the Albion the season before. It was left to Allan Glover to pierce the Palace Gates to give Albion a 1-0 win and maintain their one hundred percent start to life in the second tier of English football.

It was ever thus that the Baggies flattered to deceive. Just when The Hawthorns faithful were looking forward to the establishment of a firm promotion challenge, the side embarked on a run of ten games without a win — with some real humdinger performances amongst them! Howe chose that disastrous spell to blood an Albion youngster by the name of Barry Donaghy, once dubbed "the new Gerd Muller" by the Albion boss, who was eagerly awaiting the day that the young Geordie filled Tony Brown's boots. It was not to be.

In that spell, they lost miserably to struggling sides like Sheffield Wednesday and Preston — at home and away in the space of a week — and drew six, which gave the impression that they were hard to beat, but they could only score six goals in that period, with the dependable Brown hitting five.

In a 1-1 draw at Bristol City, Tony renewed acquaintance with Bobby Gould. Tony gave Albion the lead on 25 minutes, only for Gould to pop up with an equaliser ten minutes later. The future Albion manager stole all the headlines, as usual, by going into goal after the Bristol keeper Cashley broke his arm, and was only beaten once — when Tony gleefully smashed home a cross in the 65th minute, only to see the goal chalked off because David Shaw had strayed into an offside position.

On October 24, Albion finally ended their lean spell with a win over Sheffield Wednesday, only to crash out of the League Cup a week later — at home to Fourth Division Exeter City; the first time that a club from so low in the League ladder had won a game at The Hawthorns. What a sweet night that was for an Albion reject — and one of Tony's best mates, Campbell Crawford, who played at right back for the Greecians.

The giant-killing feat had its effect on the Albion players. Galvanised at last, perhaps by the jeers of derision from their own supporters that black night, they won five of their next six games to start climbing the table. Tony scored League goals numbers 148 and 149 in victories over Cardiff and Notts County respectively — but then went six games without a goal, as Albion relied on the new-found "Super Sub" David Shaw, who came off the bench to score in three successive games, including the match at home to Oxford when he scored the fastest goal ever scored by a substitute at that time, just twenty seconds or so after coming on.

That goal took Albion up into the highest position — fourth — they would achieve in the Second Division under Howe, and that was consolidated with a draw at promotion favourites Sunderland, which set Albion up nicely for the biggest game of the season at home to old rivals Aston Villa on Boxing Day.

The Aston men had had a torrid time of it since relegation from Division One in 1967. They had fallen into Division Three for the first time in 1970, but were at last beginning to re-emerge as a force to be reckoned with. In 1972-73 they had missed out on promotion, and the pressure on them to restore their former glory — seven championships and seven cup wins — was probably even greater than that faced by the Albion.

On Boxing Day 1973 the Villa were five places below the Albion in the League — but in this tightest of divisions, that only meant a deficit of two points. Tony has often said that he has always considered Villa to be Albion's greatest rivals, ahead of even the Wolves, and he must have relished the prospect of Albion's first League game against them in seven years. And not only was he looking for the win — he wanted that elusive 150th League goal!

Although this was the 99th League clash between the old adversaries, they had never before met outside the top flight. With a pedigree like that, it was no wonder that the game attracted over 43,000 people to The Hawthorns — the biggest gate for ANY Second Division game that season. In goal for the Villa was a familiar face. Jim Cumbes had moved to Villa Park in 1971, sold by Howe shortly after he took over at the Albion, and the match turned out to be memorable — in very different ways — for both Tony and Jim.

Tony scored Albion's first goal after 34 minutes. Cumbes blocked a shot from Glover and, miraculously, did the same again when Brown followed up, but the ball bobbed up neatly into the air for Tony to force a header over the line. It was a statistician's field day — not only Brown's 150th League goal of his career, but also the Albion's 400th in competitive football against the Villa over ninety years!

Three minutes from time, the Bomber struck again, sealing the game for Albion in front of the massed ranks of Villa supporters at the Smethwick End "the cross-shot going at half pace under Cumbes' body, as the goalkeeper went down almost in slow motion" wrote the reporter from the *Express & Star*. It would not be the last time that Cumbes gifted Albion (or Brown) a goal.

As the new year arrived, the country was in the grip of a crisis which would eventually bring down Ted Heath's Government. A coal strike meant power cuts — and power cuts meant restrictions on floodlights. As a result, kick-offs for Saturday matches were brought forward to 2 pm, and midweek games had to be played, as had always been the case before the introduction of floodlights, on midweek afternoons.

One player who wasn't on strike was the Bomber. In one week in January 1974, the city of Nottingham felt the full force of his striking prowess, in a remarkable week of scoring. On January 5, Notts County visited The Hawthorns in the third round of the FA Cup. It was the first meeting between the sides in the Cup since 1922, when County had pulled off a surprise 2-0 win; Tony made sure there was no repetition of that scoreline.

After six minutes Tony latched onto a long clearance from Latchford to drive a shot past his namesake in the County goal — only to see the ball bounce back off the post and into the keeper's arms. Three minutes later, he opened the scoring when he lashed home a shot from point blank range. Willie Johnston made it 2-0 and then, with the clock ticking away at the end of the second half, the winger released a through ball for Tony to drill a low shot into the net. In injury time, he completed his hat-trick. After teasing two defenders, he cut in from the left and scored with a low right footer. It was his first, and only, treble in the FA Cup, but it gave him a "full set" — hat-tricks in League, League Cup, Europe and the FA Cup, the only Albion man thus far — and one of the few in the history of British football — to achieve that particular feat.

A week later, it was the turn of Nottingham Forest, at the City Ground. The sides were level on points near the top of the table, both challenging for promotion, and a tough battle was expected. After ten minutes, a mix-up in the Forest defence left Tony with an open goal, to make it 1-0. Forest nearly equalised when John Wile headed against his own post, but in the 19th minute the gifted Duncan McKenzie did level for Forest with a powerful shot from ten yards. Brown continued his one-man crusade against the Lace City when he put Albion back into the lead after a clever dummy by David Shaw had sent him clear ten minutes before the break.

Two minutes into the second half, Tony made it 3-1 when he got on the end of a deflection from Shaw to score from close range, for his second consecutive hat-trick — but this time he wasn't finished, and he scored a fourth goal in the 64th minute, again from an assist by Dave Shaw. Four goals in one League game — a feat which elevated Tony up there with previous Albion greats such as W G Richardson, Jimmy Cookson, Ronnie Allen and Derek Kevan — represented the pinnacle of Tony's goalscoring career, and the *Sports Argus'* banner headline, "Wham: Terrific Tony in a solo demolition show" nicely summed up his achievement. The Forest manager, Dave Mackay, mot surprisingly, was also impressed: "Brown gets into scoring positions before you know he's there. He's so fast, you can't stop him".

The win over Forest took Albion back up to fourth place, and nicely positioned for a promotion assault. Morale and confidence were high — and they were boosted further by impressive performances against First Division Everton in the fourth round of the FA Cup. The first match was played at Goodison on January 27 — the first time that Albion had ever played a match of any sort on a Sunday — and the attendance of over 53,000 was, for many years, the biggest for a game on the Sabbath in this country.

The Second Division upstarts surprised their struggling top flight rivals, and, indeed, should have won the tie at the first attempt, had not Allan Glover shot wide of an open goal in the last minute. The replay was full of drama; and at least it was able to go ahead under floodlights, as Albion hired a generator to power the lights. On the pitch, Willie Johnston supplied all the electricity — rolling on the rain-soaked pitch and exchanging a flurry of blows with Everton defender Archie Styles. Referee J D Williams had no alternative but to send both men off — it was something that Willie was getting used to — but by then Albion had scored the goal which was to send them through into the fifth round, the Bomber keeping up his scoring run by heading home a corner in the 39th minute.

Talk was in the air of a Cup and League Double to equal the club's still unique feat of winning promotion and the FA Cup in 1931 — but then that always happened whenever Albion were in the Second Division and won a cup match! They negotiated a difficult Sunday fixture at Portsmouth, which saw David Shaw sent off before resuming their Cup exploits at home to Newcastle United in the fifth round of the cup — almost twenty years to the day from the club's famous 3-2 victory of 1954, when Ronnie Allen hit a hat-trick against the Tynesiders on the way to Wembley! There was no repeat of that scoreline. West Bromwich became Geordieland for a day as the northern hordes swamped the town, going away contented with an easy 3-0 victory inspired by Malcolm McDonald.

Undaunted, Albion's good form in the Second Division held up. A nostalgic farewell goal from Jeff Astle, who would leave for Dunstable Town at the end of the season rescued a point against Bristol City, which was followed by a 1-0 win over Alan Ashman's Carlisle at Brunton Park before the side travelled the short distance to Villa Park for the return game against their nearest neighbours.

The game was decided in an eight minute spell midway through the first half, when all four goals were scored — and it was Albion who came on top, thanks to a header from John Wile, and another two goals from Tony Brown, one a penalty at the Holte End. A sweet "double" indeed — and only the second time in ninety years of trying that an Albion side had won home and away against Villa during a League season!

When Albion made the trip to Burnden Park to play Bolton on March 9, they were fifth in the table — they always seemed to falter when they had the opportunity to get into the top three promotion slots

— but they were only two points behind second placed Luton Town, who they knew they had to face at The Hawthorns on the last Saturday of the season. Middlesbrough, managed by Jack Charlton, were runaway leaders, and looking good for the Championship.

At Bolton, Albion led after seven minutes when Astle flicked a header on to Brown who cracked in his 22nd goal of the season. This was the last time that the Astle-Brown combination resulted in a goal — and it had been three years (the "riot" game at Leeds) that the two men had both featured on the score-sheet together. Nine minutes from time, a point was squandered when John Byrom equalised for the home side, but with a home game ahead against Middlesbrough, the team sensed their chances to make a real impact in the promotion race. That's when the wheels came off.

The following Saturday, Middlesbrough came to The Hawthorns and won 4-0, in what was Jeff Astle's last full game for the Baggies, and the side never recovered from the psychological effects of that comprehensive lesson in finishing. The following Wednesday, Hull City were the visitors and Albion threw away a two goal lead to lose to an 85th minute goal from Stuart Pearson, which resulted in Howe wielding the axe for the next game at Notts County. That meant Tony missing his first game of the season, as Albion crashed to their third consecutive defeat.

Albion won just once in their seven game run-in to the season, and although Tony was soon restored to the side, he didn't manage to get on the scoresheet again until that last game at home to Luton Town. With Albion's promotion hopes long gone, it was Luton who came looking for the point that would take them back to the First Division after fifteen years away. They got it — despite a late penalty from the Bomber — and Albion had to settle for eighth place. They had picked up just six points out of a possible 33 in the last eleven games of the season; three more wins in that awful run-in would have sent them up instead of Luton...

During the season, as well as collecting another 23 goals in League and Cup, Brown had passed three new milestones. At Everton in the cup, he played his 500th first team game, whilst the replay marked his 450th League and cup game, with his 350th League game following soon after in the match at Brisbane Road. All facts and figures that were included in the matchday programme for Tony's Testimonial game at The Hawthorns on May 6 1974, which was granted to mark his ten years at the club. Unusually, the traditional rivals, Albion and Aston Villa combined for the night to take on —and beat — a combined Birmingham City/Wolves XI. Tony, of course, scored the winner in front of 12,000 appreciative fans — an attendance better than half a dozen League and Cup games on the ground, and a tremendous tribute to the contribution Tony had made to the club over the years. "I was driving down the Birmingham Road that night, on the way to the match, and I suddenly came over all emotional, because I realised all these people were coming out to see me — not the Albion, really, this match, but for me — and I choked up. It's a great thing to see, really."

Having failed in their bid to obtain promotion at the first attempt, Howe regrouped his players for a second offensive the following season. Pre-season, he took his side on a two match tour of Belgium, where they played — and lost to — John Talbut's side, FC Mechelen, before winnimg 2-1 at Diest two days later. On home turf, they then took part in the Texaco Cup, which had been revised into a group system which saw Albion win one, lose one and draw one, failing to quailfy for the knock-out stage despite thrashing Norwich City 5-1. Tony opened his account for the season with a goal in that game.

In the League, they got off to a bad start, losing the two opening, dire games, against Fulham and Hull without scoring a goal, but wins over Sunderland, at home, and Portsmouth, in a gale force wind at Fratton Park, followed, as did a win over Millwall in the League Cup.

Then it was the turn of Manchester United to visit The Hawthorns, in the first Second Division game between the clubs for 63 years. The result against the leaders ended 1-1, but the game was one of the poorest between the sides for years. Albion's form was totally uninspiring — and so was Tony's! He failed to score a goal in the League until his ninth game of the season, when he hit the opener in a 3-0 win over Oxford, and although Albion won the next two games as well, and started climbing the table at last, he was still not amongst the goals.

A sign of his new Howe-inspired role as goal-provider came when Albion won 2-0 at Cardiff on October 12, with Tony setting up both the goals. First he dived in bravely to lay on a chance for Joe Mayo and then, in the last minute, and with only the goalkeeper to beat, he unselfishly squared the ball for young Barry Donaghy to net his only Albion goal.

Form dipped again after that — six games without a win, and only one more Brown special, which led to his bring dropped to the substitute's bench. He returned to the team to notch the winner against his home town side Oldham at the end of November as the side returned to form and embarked on a run of six wins in eight games, thrusting themselves into promotion contention at last.

Four days before Christmas 1974, Villa were the visitors to The Hawthorns, but unlike the previous season, interest in the fixture had waned considerably, as the gate dipped below the 30,000 mark for the game against Ron Saunders' side. Tony certainly didn't take too much interest in it — he was firmly planted on the subs' bench for the whole ninety minutes, watching as Jim Cumbes gifted his old side an own goal to add to one from Joe Mayo as Albion won 2-0.

It was not until January that Tony got his place back in the side — for his favourite competition — scoring a goal in the fourth round of the FA Cup as Albion went down 3-2 at Carlisle. His goal was from the penalty spot — his first goal of any kind for two months in the most barren spell of his career to date — and he was dropped again until the home game with Sheffield Wednesday on March 8.

The previous week, at Sunderland, Tony had been on the bench for the tough trip to promotion favourites and FA Cup holders Sunderland. With the game goalless, the home side were awarded a penalty in the 58th minute. John Osborne, who had been carrying an injury, stunned the crowd — and the watching *Match of The Day* viewers, by pulling off his green jersey and handing it to full-back Gordon Nisbet. The two swapped shirts and Nisbet, who, of course, had made his League debut as a goalkeeper for the Albion, faced Tony Towers' penalty. The keeper turned centre-forward turned full-back turned keeper again didn't have to do a thing, as Towers hit the penalty against the post, then headed the rebound onto the bar, and out Mission accomplished, Ossie went back in goal! By then, of course, Sunderland were up for it, and they scored three quick goals. By the 84th minute, the game was all over, and Osborne left the field for good. On came Brown — but wait for it — Nisbet went back in goal, denying Tony a chance at a fourth clean sheet in goal for the club.

Back in the side, Tony scored two goals against the struggling Wednesday side on its way to the Third Division, and further goals followed against Oxford and Portsmouth as he at last found his shooting boots — just in time for the big promotion clash at Villa Park on March 29. Since the clash between the sides at The Hawthorns in December, Villa had turned their season around, and lay second in the table behind Manchester United, five points in front of Albion, who were tucked just behind the three front runners, in eighth place, but only a couple of points adrift of a promotion spot. A win at Villa would have done wonders for Albion's promotion chances.

And the Baggies drew first blood, as Tony slammed home a rising, curling shot from outside the area which Cumbes got a hand, only for the ball to bounce behind him and carry across the line. Jim Cumbes saw it from another angle. "When Tony shot, I thought I was almost on my line, but I must have crept further forward than I thought. As the shot came in, it lifted so I went to push it over the bar, but when I turned my head the ball was going in because I was so far forward!"

In the end, Cumbes' error mattered not a jot, because in the second half — shortly after Cumbes had atoned by making a point blank save to prevent Tony giving Albion a two goal lead — Villa scored three goals in six minutes to send Albion sliding to defeat in front of nearly 48,000 ecstatic Villa supporters.

Two days later, on Easter Monday, Albion lost 2-0 against Blackpool at Bloomfield, and that was the promotion challenge over. Tony kept up he re-found scoring form with two goals against Notts County, but, to be honest, nobody was interested. Crowds had dropped to around 7,000 in a backlash against the lack of success and the defensive style of play that Howe was still employing. Tony kept plugging away, though, and raised his total of goals for the season to a respectable 14 with another brace of goals against Millwall, in what turned out to be his last game of the season and — thankfully for Tony and the Albion — his last game under the management regime of Don Howe.

After the Millwall game, the club announced that they were not going to renew Howe's contract — a polite way of giving him the sack! In a departing statement to the press, after refusing to look after the side to the end of the season — Howe bemoaned Albion's envy of Villa and Birmingham City, and said that he thought the fans had turned against him "because we were relegated and because we didn't score enough goals". That seemed to sum it up in a nutshell!

Tony remembers Howe's last fling. "When Don got the sack, some of us had stayed behind after training, and were in the dressing room. In came Don, the door burst open, and he went to all the charts he had all over the wall — he was a great man for charts, with list of goalscorers, assists, and everything — and dragged all the charts off the wall, threw them all on the floor and walked out. And that was the last we ever saw of him! When Don left the club it was down and out. They could have gone right down through the divisions. There was nothing there at all; it was a disaster area, and they were lucky that they appointed the man that they did."

It was after Howe's departure that the delayed decision was made to treat a long-standing Achilles tendon problem that Tony had been suffering from, and he went into hospital for corrective surgery, which put him out for the rest of the season.

Brian Whitehouse took over as caretaker manager for the last three games, and Tony's absence from the team allowed a debut for a youngster by the name of Bryan Robson, who came in to score two goals in his three outings. Brown, despite his ups and downs throughout the season, still managed to finish as the club's top scorer, for the fifth consecutive season. It was the end of an unhappy period for Tony — but good times were just around the corner.

The Irishman Cometh

The summer of 1975 was spent in a search for the right man to take over control at The Hawthorns. There were rumours that Albion legend Ronnie Allen might return, but the move did not materialise. Instead, on June 20, Albion chairman Bert Millichip announced that the Baggies new man, to the surprise of everybody expecting another old Albion name, would be Eire international and former Leeds United great, Johnny Giles, Moreover, in a massive break from precedent, Giles, whose registration cost Albion another £48,000, would take up a dual role, rarely practised in the top two divisions, and certainly never contemplated before at the Albion, of player-manager.

Giles, who had started his career at Manchester United shortly after Munich — where his style had been avidly studied from the terraces by the young Bomber — before leaving to forge a magnificent ten year career at Elland Road, was a vastly experienced and influential player both in League and international football. With those two northern giants, he had served under two of the most successful managers in the history of the game, Matt Busby and Don Revie, and had already clocked up significant top flight managerial experience as player-manager of the Republic of Ireland side since 1973.

Millichip was well pleased with the club's acquisition. "We have proved to Albion supporters our intentions by getting Giles, a player who is worth his weight in gold. Now they can play their part in supporting us throughout next season."

Tony Brown was certainly relieved when Giles arrived. "The spirit had gone from the club by the time Don left. There was no atmosphere, the fans were really down and everything was very bleak. So they got in a new manager who was the complete opposite of Don Howe. Johnny Giles did a brilliant job, getting people to enjoy playing, playing to their strengths — I rate him so highly. When he came, he couldn't believe how everybody was so down at the club; it was terrible, he told me later. We still had some good players, but he could see that he would have to do a confidence job on us all and get us enjoying it all again, and gradually it worked."

The new man started off the pre-season training with a trip back to Ireland, with mixed results; a win over Shamrock Rovers only by virtue of an own goal, and a 1-0 defeat at part-timers Finn Harps, which hardly inspired confidence for the new season. Back in England, three games in the Anglo-Scottish Cup also saw Albion unable to set the world on fire, failing to qualify in a group comprising Mansfield, Notts County and Leicester, and things got off to an even worse start in the Second Division with a 3-0 hammering in Giles' first game as manager against Southampton at the Dell.

Tony started off at the bench in that game, a legacy of his Achilles tendon operation over the summer, even though Giles himself was missing from the midfield with injury, and Tony remembers that results were often grim at first, including a 4-0 thrashing at Fulham in front of *Match of The Day* cameras. "We got off to a bad start in '75-76, but he persevered even though the results weren't coming at first. He put me back in my old role, but I was still feeling the effects of the Don Howe period. I was way down in confidence, and I was still not an automatic choice in the first team, and in fact he left me out of his first team selection, at Southampton, but he brought me back for the next game, but I wasn't playing that well. But gradually he instilled confidence in everybody, not just myself, and brought the laughter back to the dressing room. But Johnny was very professional, and he brought the Leeds brand of professionalism to the club, but at the same time you could enjoy yourself as well."

Tony scored his first goal of the season against York, with new signing, former World Cup star Geoff Hurst putting the Albion 2-0 ahead before the Minster Men drew level to snatch a point. Soon after, elimination followed from the League Cup as Albion lost once more at Craven Cottage, and by the beginning of October Albion were nestling in the lowest position in their history, in the bottom two of the Second Division, only one point off the bottom.

Before the home game with Plymouth on October 18, Giles tried the Irish touch again, pitting his two charges, Albion and Ireland, against each other in a full scale practice match at Bisham Abbey, which Albion won 5-3, and they followed that up with a 1-0 win against the Pilgrims.

Tony's form was bad, so much so that he was relegated to the Reserves for the game against Blackpool, lining up in the following side: *Ward, Nisbet, Merrick, Trewick, Clarke, Rushbury, Glover, Brown, Edwards, Shaw, Robson. Sub: Gregson*, in his first game for the second team since September 1967. Tony was obviously stung by the demotion. "I was upset at being left out, and I decided that I'd show

John, and it was a good thing for me, because it gave me confidence." He scored twice in the first five minutes, the first a classic 25 yard shot, the second a close range tap-in, and completed his hat-trick in the 66th minute in a 6-0 demolition of the Seasiders.

The following week, when the first team were beating Plymouth in the aforementioned game, Tony was travelling north with the Reserves to beat Blackburn — and Tony made it five goals in two games with another couple at Ewood Park. His confidence was back, and he was raring to go — thanks to Giles! "In training John encouraged you to try things, training with a smile on your face, and I started to enjoy playing again. I got back in the side, scored a few goals and all of a sudden I was back to my old self. We couldn't wait to get into training in the mornings. A family atmosphere, and it was a lovely place again. The place, the offices and the dressing room had been superb before Don had arrived, and John brought that back again."

Tony was recalled to the first team in place of Hurst for the vital game against front-runners Bristol City at Ashton Gate, which proved, in many ways, to be a turning point for Giles' side. Bristol were top of the Second Division and with Albion still languishing in the lower reaches, the Robins obviously expected an easy win. Giles — and the "Brown Boys", had other ideas.

The first half was goalless, thanks to Albion's organised and disciplined team work. Try as they might, City just could not find a way through Albion's back four, and in the 71st minute Ally Brown gave Albion a deserved lead. Four minutes from the end, Tony marked his return in the way he knew best, by walking the ball round Cashley and into the net to clinch a fine 2-0 win.

The local and national press drooled over Albion's performance, the *Sunday Mercury* pointing out that "success was no fluke, built as it was on a foundation of top class teamwork, clockwork-like organisation and a never say die spirit that Bristol could not match". The Bristol manager, Alan Dicks, admitted as much. "You have to give Albion credit. They worked, ran, harried and prevented us from getting into our usual stride".

At last, Giles' methods — and new signings — had taken effect. With that win, Albion gained the impetus required to start to move forward — and the new-look, bearded Tony Brown was firmly back in the running as well. "When John brought in players like Mick Martin, Paddy Mulligan, we thought, what's going on here? But John knew both of them, from being the Ireland manager, and they were three jovial characters in the dressing room, which I think was half the reason he brought them in, for the banter and the jokes, but they all did well on the field as well, in the end."

In the next dozen games, up to the end of the year, Albion lost just thrice; but they were still seriously short of goals up front, as they had been under Howe. The difference was, the defence began to take on a formidable air about it, based on the Giles philosophy, "Keep a clean sheet, keep the ball, and you start with a point".

The highlight of the run up to Christmas was another away win at the home of promotion candidates Bolton Wanderers, on November 29. This was another game drenched in significance by the end of the season, as, in front of *Match of The Day* viewers again, Albion gave further notice that they had truly "turned the corner". A youngster called Bryan Robson came under the national gaze for the first time, playing only his second full game of the season, whilst, as the new generation came through, Geoff Hurst was ending his Football League career the same day, as a non-playing substitute.

Eighteen thousand fans at Burnden Park saw Albion forge a fifth minute lead when Tipton-born Joe Mayo headed home Tony's cross. Roy Greaves levelled after 21 minutes, but it was left to young "Robbo" to win the game for the Baggies ten minutes from time when he finished off a move started by Ally Brown. *The People* lauded the side. "Although Bolton were the promotion favourites, Albion produced most of the class. The subtlety of their passes switched from midfield to the front men who played havoc with the square Bolton defence and nobody could deny that Albion deserved their victory." — and Tony Brown was cited as Man of the Match, truly reflecting his return to form.

The following week, both Browns were on target as Albion defeated Portsmouth 3-1, to move ever closer to the promotion zone, only to lose 2-1 the following week at Luton, in a game which saw Giles sent off after an altercation with Paul Futcher. The Hatters were in desperate financial straits at the time; so much so that in a collection for the club before the game, Albion fans contributed £30 to their Fighting Fund. The charity was not reciprocated in the heated encounter that followed! Another defeat followed at home to bogey side Southampton, only for the side — inspired by Brown — to bounce back with a great win at Brian Clough's Nottingham Forest, as the local press appreciated. "Brown was again given a roving commission by Johnny Giles and how he revelled in the space. Apart from creating both goals, he had his sights set on goal himself in Albion's 2-0 win." There was no doubt that Brown was playing some of the best football of his career under the influence of the genial Giles, in stark contrast to his form in the dark days of the Don Howe regime.

And how the fans were beginning to appreciate it at last. The biggest home gate of the season so far, 20,000, turned up for the visit of Orient on Boxing Day, although it took a magnificent 30 yarder from Joe Mayo to win Albion a point against the Londoners. Full-back Paddy Mulligan, Giles' astute free transfer signing from Crystal Palace, had his toughest match of the season as he spent all of his time trying to keep up with the shirt tails of a young black winger by the name of Laurie Cunningham, who proved to be a real handful.

In the New Year, Tony committed the rare sin, for him, of missing a penalty in the home third round FA Cup tie with Carlisle United — but he followed up to net the rebound after Burleigh had parried his first effort, scoring a second goal soon after to wrap up a 3-1 win, sweet revenge for the previous season's elimination against the same opponents.

A draw at home to League leaders Sunderland was followed by a one nil win at York on January 17, and there was an interesting observation from the *Birmingham Post* concerning the watching Don Revie. "Revie cannot have failed to notice how Giles has attempted to mirror the Leeds formula in building Albion into a promotion-seeking side." The win took Albion to fifth place, only six points behind the leaders.

Back in the Cup, Albion took on Graham Taylor's Lincoln City at The Hawthorns in a fascinating clash of styles. Taylor's direct brand of football meant that the free-scoring Imps were taking the Fourth Division by storm, and they brought thousands of fans to West Bromwich, hoping that they could emulate the efforts of the side the last time to two clubs met in the Cup, when City pulled off a shock 3-1 in 1961. This time — with Tony's old mates Percy Freeman and Dick Krzywicki in the Lincoln side — they led 2-1 at the interval, only for goals from Mick Martin (who was lucky to be on the pitch after a dreadful first half foul) and Robson to rescue the Baggies, who won through 3-2.

Tony continued to score vital goals with a late winner at Stamford Bridge against Chelsea. A 4-0 defeat, in a replay, against Southampton, the eventual Cup winners, ended hopes of an extended Cup run, and not long after, on St Patrick's Day, there was also a serious set-back in the League when Bristol City came to The Hawthorns and went away with a shock 1-0 win. Albion hit the woodwork no less than five times, twice in the last two minutes, and it seemed as if Bristol, Bolton and Sunderland were slipping away at the top.

The balance was soon restored with a vital win over Bolton at The Hawthorns, and a good win, with Len Cantello playing at centre-forward — and scoring — and Portsmouth. As April blew in, Albion were fourth with six games to play. They were level with rivals Bolton, on 44 points, but five points behind leaders Bristol City, and three behind

Sunderland. Unfortunately, Bolton had a game in hand and a vastly superior goal average; Albion not only had to keep winning — they also had to hope that Bolton would slip up.

On April 3, Bolton drew 0-0 at home to Forest, so Albion's 3-0 demolition of Carlisle meant that they had reached the promotion zone at long last. Six days later, in a Friday night game, Albion lost 2-1 at Charlton, with Tony hitting an equaliser from the penalty spot. The following day, Bolton drew with Orient — level pegging again! By now, Bristol City and Sunderland had almost drawn away from the pack, and the third promotion spot seemed to be very much between Albion and Bolton, who still had that vital game in hand.

Fortunately, it was Bolton who were to crack under the pressure, as they went down 2-1 at home to bottom club York City. The following night, Albion opened up a two point gap by beating Fulham 3-1. Soon after, for their game in hand, Bolton had to make the difficult trip to Sunderland, who still needed the points in their search of the Championship — and lost. The following evening, April 20, Albion travelled to Orient, with a target set. With two games left to play for each side, Albion had the luxury of a two point lead over Bolton, but a poor goal average. Three points from their last two games would see Albion promoted. Orient's gate was boosted to nearly double their average by the travelling Albion fans, who saw their team thwarted by some brilliant goalkeeping by Orient keeper John Jackson. The game ended goalless.

The final Saturday of the season saw Bolton at Charlton, whilst Albion travelled, to all places, Tony's birthplace of Oldham knowing that a win would see them back in the top flight, whatever happened at the Valley. April 26 is a date enshrined in Albion's long history — it is certainly a day that Tony Brown will never forget. Over 15,000 Albion fans made the journey north. The *Match of The Day* cameras, in expectation of a gripping finish to the season, were there, the sun shone, and Boundary Park was a cauldron of noise and a sea of colour — blue and white, yellow and green as the Albion hordes took over the ground.

Oldham kicked off towards the massed ranks of Albion fans at the open end of the ground. On a hard, dusty pitch, with so much at stake for the Albion, at least, the tackling was fierce, with Cantello barracked continuously for an uncompromising tackle on Chapman which saw the Oldham midfielder carried off; his replacement, Branagan, was promptly booked for a retaliatory tackle on Giles. At the break, there was no score, but the news was filtering through — although not through the *cordon sanitaire* around the Albion dressing room — that Bolton were winning at Charlton.

Fate decreed that the game would be won in the most dramatic fashion. In the 55th minute Mulligan fed Martin on the right and his cross was headed down by Ally Brown at the far post. Tony Brown cushioned the ball on his right foot, switched it to his left and volleyed into the top corner. Tony went wild, the rest of the team went wild — and 15,000 Albion fanatics went wild!

The rest of the game was played out in a dream-like atmosphere, with Albion keeping possession as much as they could. Real drama came in the last minute when David Shaw — who Giles had released two months earlier — flicked a header goalwards only to see John Osborne pull off a thrilling save. When the final whistle went soon after, thousands of Albion fans waded onto the pitch and set up camp there, demanding that their heroes come out of the dressing room to acknowledge their great victory, and their return to the First Division after three long years in the wilderness.

Tony remembers it all as if it were yesterday. "It was as memorable as the Cup Final, that day. When the lads came out of the tunnel, we all had the shock of our lives when we saw the support we had that day. We didn't realise and that hit us — we had to do it for the thousands that had come up there. It was a great feeling winning that game, and great celebrations afterwards. We dominated the game, by having an awful lot of possession, which was Johnny's game — if you have possession, you don't give goals away. We had twenty-odd clean sheets

The most important goal of Tony's long career — the winner at Oldham in 1976, which took Albion back to the top flight

that season, which was a new club record for Ossie in goal, and if we scored a goal, we were confident that we could hold out. The winner was one of my best goals, because I brought the cross down with one foot, cushioned it and banged it in with the other. A brilliant day!"

At the time, John Wile praised Tony's contribution. "It was fitting that Tony should score the goal in his native town, because he is as loyal a servant as Albion have ever had. I doubt that he will draw more satisfaction out of any of the many goals he has scored for the club". All told, Tony played 37 League games (plus three as sub) in 1975-76, scoring just eight goals — but the eighth was probably worth eight hundred to Tony, the club and its supporters!

Albion — and Tony — back at the top

In the last week of July 1976, with the club and its supporters still basking in the glory of promotion, Johnny Giles dropped an unexpected bombshell. He tendered his resignation to the board. In a press statement Giles made his position clear. "I didn't take the decision lightly, but I feel my future lies outside Football League management". Giles still had two of his three year contract to run and, after a monumental effort by chairman Bert Millichip, Giles back-tracked "for the time being" and the club, was able to announce, on July 31, that he had changed his mind. It was certainly a relief to Tony Brown, who, under Giles, was enjoying a renaissance in his playing career. "After turning the club round, John said he was going. We couldn't believe it! But he was always his own man, right from the start, and he said he was determined to go — and then he changed his mind, and we were so pleased."

Albion were due to make a return to Ireland for a pre-season tour, but the Troubles — and the players' wives — intervened and the trip was cancelled. Instead, there was a first-ever trip to Gresty Road, Crewe, where Tony scored a penalty in a 6-2 win, followed by another go at the Anglo-Scottish Cup, where they failed to progress beyond the Group stage.

"In the First Division, everybody thought we were going to come straight back down again, but we shocked everybody — shocked ourselves, I think." There was a mouth-watering start to the League season, with an opening day trip to Giles' old club, Leeds. The little Irishman led Albion onto the pitch, and back into the First Division, to a standing ovation from the Yorkshire crowd — who were stunned into silence when Albion took a fifth minute lead through Ally Brown. Right on half time, Tony popped up to make it 2-0, powering a Joe Mayo flick past Harvey. In a second half of unrelenting pressure Albion held out until the last seven minutes when two goals gave Leeds a point.

First Division football returned to The Hawthorns four days later with a full house for the visit of Champions Liverpool, with the Keegan-Toshack double act giving the Reds a narrow victory. A week later, though, Albion went to Anfield in the League Cup and grabbed a draw, beating Liverpool in the replay with a goal from Mick Martin.

On the transfer front, Giles, believing that neither Mayo nor Ian Edwards were good enough to play consistently at the top flight, went out to sign an old friend of Tony's on a free from Preston. Ray Treacy was, in effect, returning home, having started his football career at The Hawthorns in 1964, and had played many times alongside Tony in the Reserves during that period. Now he was an international team mate of Giles', with over ten years' experience as a striker, and he fitted in well into the current side, scoring on his "debut" at Derby, as he had done in his first debut a decade before.

In the League, St Andrews was the next port of call for the Albion, and the game was won on the hour by a Tony Brown "Special" — which, in this particular season, were few and far between. Tony launched a thirty yard shot which flew into the top corner past a startled Dave Latchford, and won Albion both points against Blues on what has always been a favourite Albion hunting ground.

Memorable as that goal was, there was an even more important occasion during the game against Coventry City on Friday September 17. In the programme for the match against the Sky Blues, the Albion announced: "Tonight Tony Brown plays in his 455th League game for the club, and thus equals Jesse Pennington's club record, which has stood since April 1922." Tony had a quiet game, and it was down to John Wile to score the goal which gave Albion a point in a 1-1 draw.

Tony was back in the scoring stakes for the visit of Tottenham — already the recipients of two Bomber hat-tricks in the past — on October 2, in one of the games of the season, although that would not have been the opinion of Albion fans at half time, as struggling Spurs led 2-0. In the second half, it was Albion's turn to stage a comeback, thanks to the speed, skill and imagination of Willie Johnston.

In the 53rd minute he wriggled past three defenders before crossing into the box, where Stead handled the ball, the dependable Tony slamming in the penalty kick for his fourth goal of the season. After 64 minutes, Albion levelled when Mick Martin scored with a beautiful diving header from Cantello's cross. Roared on by their fanatical support at the Birmingham Road end, the Baggies went in for the kill. Ray Treacy scored the third, after Tony had had a shot blocked and Martin the fourth, two minutes from time, from another Johnston cross.

If that game was a classic, then the following home match, against Manchester United, finally made people sit up and realise that Albion really were back at the top, and were no soft touches. The BBC knew they were on to a good thing, and had the *Match of the Day* cameras there to record a stunning opener from Giles in the opening minutes, a terrific spinning shot from twenty yards, against his first League club.

That was to be the 99th — and last — League goal of Giles' long career. Further efforts from Ally Brown, Cantello, and Treacy wrapped up a 4-0 win which had Giles crowing, "This victory confirms we are a First Division side playing First Division football, and can meet the best in the land on equal terms."

The win took Albion as high as fifth in the table — a clear indication that Tony — and the Albion — were back where they belonged. Or so it seemed. Between October 23 and February 22, Albion won just three out of fifteen games and Tony, suffering along with the rest of the team, scored just twice. There were some real ups and downs. On November 6, the side went down to their worst defeat since that Best-inspired drubbing at Old Trafford in 1970, when Ipswich Town hit seven past a luckless John Osborne. Trevor Whymark scored four, and there was another from Paul Mariner, on his home debut for Town after turning down a move to The Hawthorns.

The following Wednesday, Albion played Aston Villa at home. Tony was presented with a solid silver team service in recognition of beating Pennington's long-standing record. Albion played worse that they had against Ipswich, but still managed to salvage a point thanks to John Wile's injury time header in a 1-1 draw. During the bad spell, Tony broke the all-time (including War-time games) Albion appearance record previously held by Len Millard — that game at Ipswich was his 627th fist team appearance!

On December 18, Tony witnessed one of the best debuts he has ever seen from an Albion player. "Derek Statham. He was a brilliant player — and what a debut he had against Stoke. He could do anything with the ball. He went off down the wing on a fifty yard run and ended up scoring a fantastic goal past Peter Shilton!"

That was the one high point in a dreadful run which also saw the Albion lose a home FA Cup replay (against Manchester City) for the first time since 1949, go down 6-1 at Roker Park to relegation-threatened Sunderland, and, worst of all, permanently lose the services of full-back Ray Wilson, who had been forced to give up the game through injury.

By this point, Albion had slipped into the bottom half of the table, and seemingly had lost all hopes of a place in Europe which had seemed a reasonable target before Christmas, but things suddenly changes thanks, mainly, to the emergence of two men. One was Bryan Robson, who returned to the side after breaking his leg in that 4-2 win over Spurs.

The other catalyst for improvement was a new signing, Laurie Cunningham. Giles had signed him from Orient on March 7 on the recommendation of new Chief Scout Ronnie Allen, in a player exchange deal which saw £110,000 and both Joe Mayo and Allan Glover going to Brisbane Road in exchange. "Laurie made quite an impact. A tremendous player, with great pace and great skill. A quiet lad, in the dressing room, but he fitted in with the rest of the side very well."

Cunningham made his debut for the Albion in a 2-0 win at Tottenham on March 12. Four days later, Albion gained revenge for that Portman Road drubbing by beating Bobby Robson's Ipswich 4-0, with Bryan Robson scoring his first League hat-trick, and Cunningham scoring his first goal for his new club — and the defeat knocked Ipswich off the top of the First Division table.

Tony was injured in the Ipswich game, and, as a result, spent the next five games on the bench, including a fine 2-2 draw at Old Trafford. He returned to the fray in the home game against Manchester City in the most unfortunate of circumstances — as a substitute for poor Robson, who broke his leg for the THIRD time that season!

At that point in the season, there were still rumours flying about concerning Giles' future at the club. That, coupled with the loss of Robson, soon had a detrimental effect on Albion's formed, which dipped once again, and they won just two of the last seven games, to miss out on that European place. After a 1-1 draw at Highfield Road on April 19, Giles publicly announced that he would definitely leave the club at the end of the season. "Ever since moving to West Bromwich in 1975 I have come to realise more and more that a Football League manager's job is impossible for me under the present system."

Tony, who had suffered so badly under the Howe regime, felt Giles' departure more than most. "We had another great shock when Johnny Giles left. It was a terrible time, because the players loved him. He brought everybody laughing again, the players, the office staff, the laundry staff — everybody at the club — and then he went The players got up a delegation, three of us, me, John Wile and Ally Robertson, went to see him to try to persuade him to change his mind, but he was adamant. John Wile spoke to the Board as well, and had a chat with the chairman: 'Try everything that you can to keep him; the players think the world of him'. But he wouldn't budge; it was always the end of the story once he's made his mind up. When he came in to say good-bye, there was complete silence, and everybody was gutted. There were tears in some players' eyes — a terrible day."

There was still time for one fabulous swan song from the little maestro. On May 7 Albion produced a champagne performance at Filbert Street against high-riding Leicester City, which showed just how much they would miss Giles in midfield. The result — 5-0 to the Albion —

was stunning enough; but the performance was even better. And Tony was there, weighing in with the fifth goal, a close range effort nine minutes from time. The *Express & Star* drooled over Giles. "The little man's brain must be like a computer for the way he picked out players on Saturday needed radar, as well as a cultured pass. When he is in full swing the opposition are chasing shadows. But more important as much to Giles as anyone was the way his colleagues responded, despite the fact that he now has only three games left in Albion colours." Giles' last act at the club was to release Ray Treacy, Steve Lynex, Colin Gregson and Derek Hood — and to pay just £5,000 for Cyrille Regis, which has to be one of the bargains of all time!

In Giles' final match at Villa Park, his side — not helped by Laurie Cunningham going "walkabout" — lost 4-0, and Giles was gone. Not for good, although no-one — including Tony Brown, who would have the opportunity to work with the Irishman once more — knew that at the time.

In the summer of 1977, Tony Pawson, the former Charlton and Pegasus amateur was the author of a book called *The Goalscorers*, in which he talked at length about Tony. "Tony Brown is another of those players whose one cap in 1971 seems an insult to his ability. With more than 180 goals for W.B.A. by the start of 1977, he has more goals for one club than anyone else still playing. To me he has always seemed to have many of the qualities of Martin Peters. Brown is a strong and accurate finisher with a fine sense of anticipation. He is particularly dangerous with his runs from deep positions, for he times them so well and has the acceleration to get into position before he can be picked up. Perhaps he has been too consistent and too unobtrusive to win much international recognition despite his high skills."

In fact, closer inspection of the record books shows that prior to the 1977-78 season, Tony stood sixth in the list of all-time goalscorers still playing at that time. His tally of 187 League goals was only bettered by Kevin Hector, Ted MacDougall, Brian Clarke, Allan Clarke and Jack Howarth. Where Tony gained precedence over all of those names was that all of his goals had been scored in the top two divisions!

Brown was chasing Ronnie Allen's club goal-scoring record, having surpassed "Peerless" Pennington's appearance total. It looked a tall order, though, as Tony had only scored eight goals in each of the previous two seasons; with 22 needed to pass Allen's total of 208, the record seemed a long, long way off.

Ironically, the new manager appointed to take control of the Albion on June 23 1977, was Ronnie Allen! He had, of course, actually rejoined the club in 1976-77, as Chief Scout/consultant, so it was really an appointment "from within". As a dashing forward, with his film star looks, he had been the hero of the Albion fans as a player throughout the Fifties. He had had some success as a manager with the Wolves and Athletico Bilbao, and now he was coming home. "Ronnie had a different appraoch to John. Perhaps it was just having come from Spain, but he wanted to see more individual play, to get the ball forward a lot quicker and to do more attacking — less possession football, which was what Giles liked so much."

Tony missed the pre-season photograph that year, because of an illness in the family, but by the time Albion travelled to Glasgow to take part in the Tennant-Caledonian Cup, he was ready and waiting to fire on all cylinders once more. Four teams took part in the invitation tournament, staged at Ibrox Park, and Albion took on St Mirren (then managed by Alex Ferguson) in the first semi-final. For the umpteenth time, it was Brown who scored Albion's first goal of the season with a 12th minute penalty kick, and he later scored another goal as Albion won 4-3. The following day, Albion met Glasgow Rangers in the Final — yet Tony, despite his two goals, was not selected. Albion, with Laurie Cunningham named Player of the Tournament, won 2-0, and took home the silverware.

Tony was very much back in the side for the opening League game of the season at The Hawthorns against newly-promoted Chelsea, and he made his presence felt with two goals, including a penalty, in a 3-0 win. That was followed by a 2-2 draw at Elland Road — when the side recovered from a two goal deficit — and a 3-0 hammering at Anfield as Kenny Dalglish celebrated his move from Celtic. Tony was injured in that game, a setback which inadvertently helped Cyrille Regis launch His Albion career. With both Tony and centre-forward David Cross out, the £5,000 bargain from Hayes was chosen to play in the next game, at home to Rotherham in the League Cup. Two goals ahead, Albion were awarded a penalty, and, with Tony missing, the crowd chanted for the 19 year old to step up and take the kick — and a new legend was born, as "Smokin' Joe" scored from the spot, and added a second before the end to complete a 4-0 win.

Cyrille was on target once again with a wonder goal to beat Middlesbrough on the Saturday — but Tony missed that one as well, the only League game that he failed to start during the season. But he remembers the goal which marked the arrival of a prodigious new talent. "A fantastic goal, the way the youngster beat three experienced Middlesbrough defenders so easily — incredible, really, for a lad from non-League."

By the time the side travelled north to play — and beat — Newcastle at St James' Park, Tony was firmly ensconced in the side, as Albion lost just twice in eleven games. And Tony was back on the goal-scoring trail just as in days of old, with seven goals in that spell. They included two goals against Birmingham City in front of the *Match of The Day* cameras, both goals in a 2-1 win at Coventry the week after, and a Bonfire Night goal in a 2-0 win over Leicester — when he also missed a penalty.

Sandwiched in all this was another cracking "Bomber Special" against Watford in the League Cup. Although outplayed by Graham Taylor's outfit, Albion dispatched them with another moment of Bomber magic. "Brown's 52nd minute match-winner, rifled in on the run and at an angle from twenty yards was the one and only way Albion could find to dismiss a splendid Watford side."

As a result of that win against Leicester on November 5, Albion went third in the First Division, just three points behind Nottingham Forest. Just when a challenge for the championship looked on, Albion — and Tony — forgot how to score goals! A mystifying slump arrived, with five successive draws, four of them goalless, plus an embarrassing 1-0 defeat at Bury in the League Cup, on a freezing foggy night when nothing went right.

It was a warmer evening on December 13, when Albion flew out to Saudi Arabia for a lucrative friendly against their national side in Dhahran. It was an ominous game — whilst Tony was cracking the winner, Ronnie Allen was in negotiations with the Saudi Prince to take over as the country's national coach. Everybody was flabbergasted when, three days before Christmas 1977, Allen — who still had not been given a contract by the Albion board — left for the lure of petrodollars. John Wile was appointed in a caretaker capacity until a new boss could be found, and there was some call for the popular centre-half to be given the job permanently.

Wile was in charge for five games, which included two 3-1 defeats in succession at Bristol City and at home to Arsenal over the holiday period. On the last day of the year, Albion were at home to Leeds, and they fairly peppered the United goal, only for Dave Stewart in the visitors' goal to keep them at bay — until five minutes from the end. Mick Martin was fouled in the area and Tony belted home the spot kick to give Wile his only win as caretaker boss.

On New Year's Day Tony scored a last minute equaliser in a 2-2 draw at Chelsea — and was Wile a relieved man! "I couldn't have wished for a better bloke to be in that position at that moment." The *Evening Mail* was also appreciative of Tony's efforts that afternoon.

"Brown spent the afternoon running around Stamford Bridge as if he were on the way to his 60th appearance instead of his 600th." It was definitely a case of "Carry on Regardless" as far as Tony was concerned, whoever the manager might be. For the club, it was a case of out with the old, and in with the new.

In the FA Cup third round game at home to Blackpool, Tony approached his favourite competition with renewed vigour, scoring from the spot past his old mate Bob Ward in a 4-1 win. "That was only the second time I ever tried to place the ball from a penalty, because normally I hit them as hard as I could. I missed one against United in 1972 when I placed the ball wide of the post. Bob Ward, the ex-Albion youngster, was in goal. Because he knew all about my penalty style, banging it as hard as I could down the middle, I changed my style and rolled it into the corner, as he stood his ground expecting the usual 'You bastard!' was all Bob could say as he picked the ball out of the net!" Then Ron Atkinson arrived as manager — and what a fillip for the club he turned out to be!

"Ronnie Allen kept us doing the same things, but we missed Johnny Giles on the pitch. Then Ron Atkinson came in, and nobody knew who he was at the time. A big fellow, bubbly character, he came striding in and introduced himself, and said 'Let's get onto that training pitch and get playing!' The pre-match wind-up in the dressing room is absolutely vital, and most of it is down to the manager. I've played for a lot of managers at the Albion — about one every two years when I was playing, which proves something in itself. Whatever you think of Ron Atkinson, he was a brilliant motivator. He used to punch you down the tunnel, you know. He'd whack you, and say, 'Go on, get out there and entertain all those people. And I'm one of them — and I want to be entertained as well!' You just couldn't wait to get out after that."

Atkinson had been a powerful wing-half with Oxford United in his playing days. As a manager he had done very well at Kettering and Cambridge United, but he was quite a gamble for the Albion — a gamble that was, however, to pay glorious dividends, in terms of entertainment and quality play, if not actual trophies. "Ron would take us for five-a-side and one day he'd be Denis Law, the next he'd be Beckenbauer, and the next he'd be Pele. It was just like you were as a kid. He was that enthusiastic, and the dressing room was just a happy place to be. Yet he'd come from nowhere, and he was only 42 — what a job it must have been for him."

After losing in his first game in charge, Atkinson took his team to Old Trafford for the fourth round of the FA Cup — against the holders. A game of outstanding thrills, played in front of 57,000 fans, ended 1-1.

Albion scored in the 78th minute, when Ally Brown centred for his namesake Tony to head down into the penalty area for Johnston to net. With the Stretford End, Tony's old terrace home, silenced, Albion appeared to be heading for a memorable win until, in the last minute, Steve Coppell equalised with a twenty yarder which hit the post and rebounded into the net off keeper Tony Godden's back.

If the first game had been a classic, then the replay truly exceeded all expectations. An all-ticket crowd of 38,000 gathered in the pouring rain to watch another breathtaking spectacle of all-out attack from both sides. Ray Matts captured the mood in the *Birmingham Mail;* "It was a game that grabbed you by your emotions, jangled you up with a wonderful assortment of skills, incident and high drama and left you mentally drained. But oh, so contented at money well spent."

And, as usual, Tony was in there with his usual goal against United. In the eleventh minute Ally Brown headed a Willie Johnston cross into Tony Brown's pass, and his fierce volley whistled past Paddy Roche, only for Stuart Pearson to equalise for the Cup holders nine minutes later.

Four minutes into the second half, big Cyrille Regis made it 2-1, tapping in after a Willie Johnston shot had hit the bar. On the hour, an awful challenge from Joe Jordan fractured John Wile's cheekbone and the defence, already without the suspended Ally Robertson, had to regroup, with Mick Martin moving back to play at centre back alongside Bryan Robson. The pair of them played brilliantly, holding back United's constant attacks, but, in the last minute, the visitors equalised once again. It was a carbon copy of their late leveller at Old Trafford, except that this time it was Gordon Hill's shot that beat Godden, hit the post — and bounced back into the net off the luckless goalkeeper's

Into the second century of goals — from the spot, at Ipswich again

body! But it was to be Albion's night — twenty eight seconds into extra time, Johnston hit the bar once more, and Regis headed in the rebound to win the game.

In the bread and butter of the League, Tony notched another career milestone on February 28 at St Andrews, when he became one of that select players in the one hundred year history of the Football League to reach the 200 goal mark, in Albion's 2-1 win over the Blues. A long clearance by Godden was headed on by Regis to Tony, who swept down the middle to reach his double century. In the next match, Tony scored twice against Ipswich at Portman Road, the second yet another last minute equaliser.

Back in the Cup, Albion had already pulled off a stunning 3-2 win at Derby — their only peacetime win at the Baseball Ground in the last seventy years of its existence — and went one better when they ended Nottingham Forest's long, long unbeaten run with a 2-0 Hawthorns win at the quarter-final stage, to earn a semi-final meeting with Ipswich at Highbury.

Albion were certainly on a roll. They lost just once in the six games prior to the big Cup meeting on April 8 1978 and were favourites to win against Ipswich, still managed by the man Tony had watched playing in the blue and white stripes on his rare days off from apprentice football back in 1961. Bobby Robson was most specific before the game on who he thought was Albion's danger man. "We MUST be wary of Tony Brown. His late runs from midfield are a real danger. His finishing is deadly and if were are not vigilant he could well be the man to destroy us."

Much has been said on the reasons why Albion lost that game — Ron Atkinson foolishly wound up the Ipswich team by appearing on *Football Focus* before the game, walking around Wembley; they "froze" on the day; Willie Johnston dislocated his shoulder; John Wile gashed his head open in a clash with Brian Talbot; Mick Martin was sent off — after a veritable catalogue of disasters, but for Tony, that semi-final defeat was the worst moment of his long career. "Ron was confident that we'd win the Cup, because we were such a great side. I scored a penalty, and for a minute there was a flicker that we might get back into it, but then Mick Martin got sent off... it was the worst day of my life, another one of those days. You're so close in the semi-final, which is why I actually rate my greatest disappointment as losing in the semi-finals in 1978, because, as well as everything else, I was coming to the end of my career. It was the last chance saloon for me. I thought, 'End of my career, I'm going to have a Wembley Final', so it was doubly disappointing then. Bobby Robson came in the dressing room afterwards — because I knew him from my early days at the Albion — and he put his arm round me and said 'Bad luck, it wasn't your day'; but we didn't need that, to be honest"

After the disappointment, Albion buckled down to lose just once in the last seven games. "The team picked itself still, although Ron has said that he always intended to change the side, but it was doing so well that he didn't have to; once again, the dressing room was absolutely brilliant under Ron." The last game of the season was played out at home to Nottingham Forest who, by the time they arrived at The Hawthorns, had already secured the League Championship. In a 2-2 draw, Tony netted his 19th League goal of the season, to finish as the club's top scorer by a mile. It was his 206th goal, taking him ever closer

Losing a semi-final can be painful, especially at the "last chance saloon"

to Allen's record, and true Albion immortality.

Albion's long, epic season was still not over, however. In May they became the first Western side ever to tour China. Playing four games in the People's Republic, and one in Hong Kong, they remained unbeaten, and Tony went oriental with goals against Kwanjung Province and Hong Kong. Tony was less than impressed with the honour conferred on the club by the invitation to tour. "Hong Kong — now that was some place — I've never seen anything like it. China was so bad — I've never seen poverty like it; it was unbelievable. We wanted to go home after the first day; you couldn't get a drink, for a start, there were no cars, there was nothing at all to do. We were streaming into Ron Atkinson's room and asking him if he could get us home early. It was like hell on earth, honestly. They used to lock the corridors of the hotels at night, so you couldn't go anywhere. When we got off the train at the border, at Hong Kong, it was the quickest the lads had ever run, faster than any match they'd ever played in, as they ran over than border — it was like being free after being in prison!"

Eventually, Tony returned home. John Osborne retired, which meant that Tony was the last remaining member of the great 1968 FA Cup winning side. Willie Johnston was "busted" in Argentina in the glare of the World Cup but for Tony, there was still time for one more season in the sun.

The assault on the Championship

The pre-season warm-up dreamed up by Ron Atkinson in August 1978 went from the sublime to the ridiculous. The schedule started at Fir Park, Motherwell for a Testimonial game for Joe Wark, brother of the free-scoring Ipswich midfielder. Amazingly, and surely a sign of things to come that season, Albion brushed aside the Scots to the tune of eight goals to one — both Ally Brown and Cunningham scored hat-tricks, but Tony weighed in with a goal and, most notably, in the Albion goal for half the match was a young Rhodesian goalkeeper looking for a work permit — one Bruce Grobbelaar.

The squad then moved on across to Ibrox Park, Glasgow, to defend their Tennant-Caledonian Cup which they had won a year before by beating the host club in the Final. There was to be no repeat, as Albion were drawn against fellow First Division side Southampton in the first game, and lost 3-1 on penalties, with — naturally — Tony Brown the only Albion man to find the net in the penalty shoot-out. The Third Place Play-off game the following day against Hearts was lost 2-0.

From Glasgow — to Syria! The Albion trekked off to one of football's forgotten outposts to play two matches, against a Northern Syrian Provincial side, and against the Damascus Police XI, Tony popping up with a goal in a 1-1 draw against the latter side in front of 12,500 fans.

The trip to Syria was more memorable for the return journey, rather than the quality of the opposition. On August 14, the *Sandwell Mail* reported; "Albion players and officials survived a landing scare during the tour in Syria. Returning to Damascus airport after their first game, the overloaded army plane struck the runway with a frightening jolt. The plane had been overloaded after picking up a Tunisian basketball team. 'Everyone was sitting on top of each other and there were even people sitting on top of the team's travel kit' said Albion director Sid Lucas."

The team survived — and were soon back home in readiness for the start of the new season on August 19, when Albion kicked off with a "revenge" match at home to FA Cup holders Ipswich Town, victors over Albion in that dramatic Highbury semi-final only four months before. Little did Tony know as he kicked off in that game that the

August sunshine heralded the final full campaign that he would share with the Albion.

For Tony, though, as Albion's top scorer in 1977-78, it was business as usual, as he started the season by scoring the decisive second goal, with a scrambled effort that went in off the crossbar. Tony vehemently claimed the goal despite some argument at the time that George Burley had put the ball past his own goalkeeper. Tony put his case after the game. "Paul Cooper was out of goal and I ran forward and got in a header. That hit the woodwork but the crux of the matter is, in my opinion, George Burley only helped the ball into the net when it rebounded off the bar. My goal — of that I am sure, and I understand from the Boss that the club are officially giving it to me!" Another notch on Tony's belt, on the way to beating Ronnie Allen's record.

It had been a sizzling start to the season all round, for Albion's first goal, from the boot of Ally Brown, had been scored after just 22 seconds — the first goal of the new season anywhere in the Football League — and that momentum was carried through as the Baggies won their first three games in the First Division, something that the club had not achieved for over forty years. However, Tony picked up an injury in the 4-0 defeat of newly promoted Bolton Wanderers at The Hawthorns, and proceeded to miss the next eight League and Cup games. He was certainly missed, as Albion slumped, winning just twice. They were dumped out of the League Cup after a three match epic against Leeds United that only ended after Albion had had Len Cantello sent off in the second replay at neutral Maine Road.

The two matches that Albion did win were against lightweight foreign opposition, as they beat Turkish side Galatasaray in the Albion's first tie in Europe for nigh on a decade, winning 3-1 at home and away in the UEFA Cup first round tie. Although Tony missed the torrid trip to Izmir for the first leg, he was back as a second half substitute for the home leg on September 27. "Ron had sent Colin Addison over to Turkey to spy on Galatasaray before the tie. We were all in the dressing room and Ron called for the huge file that Colin had drawn up. He took it — and ripped it in half and threw it on the floor! 'They're rubbish — we don't need this, because they need to worry about us more than we need to worry about them'. Colin's face was a picture, when he saw what was happening to all that work and travel that he'd put in!"

Three days later, Tony was back in the side for the trip to Stamford Bridge, replacing Willie Johnston in Albion's talent-packed squad. refreshed and renewed, he played his part in a fine Albion performance, as well as scoring a goal of great significance. Albion needed a win to keep up with the early season leaders, but went behind after just four minutes to a Chelsea side that was still without a home win. Cyrille Regis levelled matters in the 21st minute to make the score 1-1 at the break, and two goals in two second half minutes gave Albion the vital points.

The first goal came from a Wile header from a Tony Brown corner kick — but the second was far more important; the one that everybody associated with the club had been waiting for. On 59 minutes, Albion were awarded a free kick and Chelsea (and the Star Soccer camera team, who lamentably missed the goal) were caught napping. As Bryan Robson took the kick quickly, chipping the ball into Bomber's path, Brown joyfully smashed a left foot shot past Bonetti to equal Ronnie Allen's goal-scoring record — the 208th League goal of Tony's career!

The stage was set the following week, again in front of the BBC cameras, for Tony to make the record his own, as Albion turned out against another newly-promoted side, Tottenham. A club that Tony had always scored freely against in the past, they — Ardiles and Villa notwithstanding — were struggling near the bottom of the table, having just lost 7-0 at Anfield to most people's title favourites, Liverpool. Against all expectations, Spurs scored in the fourth minute with what was virtually their only shot of the game and for all the pressure that Albion applied, they couldn't find the net. Albion dropped as low as sixth and Tony had to travel to Leeds in search of "that" goal.

Once again, at Elland Road, on October 14, Leeds went behind to an early goal, scored by Byrom Stevenson. Six minutes before the interval, Tony Brown created the Albion goal-scoring record which will almost certainly never be beaten. He picked up a loose ball in midfield and was still 25 yards out from goal when he beat David Harvey with a great strike, the ball entering the net off the post. Two further goals, both set up by the wizardry of Willie Johnston completed Albion's first win on the ground since the infamous "riot" match in 1971.

It's there! League goal number 209 goes in at Elland Road, and Tony Brown officially takes over from Ronnie Allen as the Albion's greatest ever goalscorer

In the following week's programme notes in the *Albion News*, for the game against Coventry City, Ron Atkinson added his congratulations to all the others for Tony's achievement. "I would like to congratulate Tony Brown on establishing a new record for Albion. His goal against Leeds, I am sure you all know, set a new record of 209 League goals for the club and it surely is a tremendous feat." Before the kick-off, Albion and City players formed a guard of honour on the pitch, as Tony was presented with the ball from the Leeds game, with which he had scored the record-breaking goal, by Albion chairman Bert Millichip.

Prior to the game against the Sky Blues, Albion had made more progress in Europe, beating Portugal side Sporting Braga 1-0 away from home — but that was a mere warm-up for the game against Coventry, in which, for the first time that season, Albion showed a truly ruthless streak. City forsook their normal sky blue strip for a ghastly chocolate coloured concoction that had the wits on the terraces in fine voice — but the Chocolate Men soon melted in the face of a blistering attacking performance from a fearsome Albion side. By the break, the game was all but settled, as Albion led 3-0, but four

Before the home game with Coventry (7-1!) Bert Millichip presents the ball with which Tony scored his record-breaking 209th goal against Leeds United

more goals followed as Albion ran riot in the second half. Tony scored the fifth — a screaming right footer from twenty yards — as well has having another perfectly good goal chalked off in the last minute, with the score at 7-1.

By now, Albion were on a roll. During the month of November, they were unbeaten in six matches, including four successive 1-0 wins over Braga (again), Birmingham, Ipswich and Bolton, before they took on their greatest challenge of the season so far, with a third round UEFA Cup first leg game at the home of Valencia. The Spaniards were one of the favourites to win the competition, and could sport World Cup stars Kempes and Bonhof in their star-studded side — but they could not beat an Albion side inspired by a once in a lifetime performance from Laurie Cunningham. Tony missed the first leg, but travelled with the party. "I missed the Valencia away game, with that old back strain again, but I watched it from the stand in Valencia that night, and Laurie Cunningham was absolutely brilliant that day, and no wonder Real Madrid sat up and took notice; a great one-man performance. I was fit again for the second leg, and scored both the goals, and it was a great thing for us to beat Valencia, a great scalp for the club, as they had Bonhof and Kempes in the side, and it showed that we could compete with the top teams in Europe."

Indeed, that night of floodlit glory against Valencia has gone down as one of the greatest in the Albion's history. Thirty four thousand fans braved the freezing conditions to see a memorable performance summed up by the *Evening Mail.* "And then there was Tony Brown. Twice he struck with lethal certainty to win the tie. First with a fifth minute penalty, which had Valencia manager Marcelo Domingo screaming at referee Robert Wurtz in the tunnel after the game... then with a 79th minute right foot volley which must rate among the very best of his two hundred plus goals." In fact, it could have been even better, as Tony was robbed of a deserved final hat-trick for the club by the referee, who ruled out another good effort because of handball by Cyrille Regis.

On a night when the team took all the plaudits, John Wile appreciated the importance of Tony's early strike. "There's no substitute for experience, and that's why I had every confidence in Tony Brown as he stepped up to take the vital penalty. It is a fact that more penalties are scored than missed, but in a match like this one, the pressure on Bomber was enormous. For a start, there was the importance of getting an early lead. There was the electric atmosphere to take into account, and then there's the choice of which side to place the kick — and then, suddenly, yards diminish to feet. Tony also had to wait until the inevitable

Valencia protests had been brushed aside by the referee, before he was able to shoot us into the lead."

On went Albion's unbeaten run, with further wins against Middlesbrough and Wolves — the last a tremendous 3-0 win at Molineux where Tony scored another well-received 25 yarder against a struggling Wolves side. But there was an ill-wind blowing — the first signs of winter, which would do so much to ruin Albion's chances of their first League Championship for nearly sixty years, arrived on Friday December 22, when Albion's home game with Southampton was snowed off.

With the nation firmly in the grip of the worst winter since the "Deep Freeze" of 1962-63, it took the undersoil heating at Highbury to ensure that the Boxing Day match at Highbury could go ahead. This, surely, was the result that made the football pundits sit up and take notice — yet the game has always been overshadowed by another, fantastic win four days later.

Before the game in north London, Albion were third, ahead of Arsenal only on goal average, whilst the Gunners were fresh from a astonishing 5-0 win at White Hart Lane three days before (the match which featured Liam Brady's famous "banana shot" goal). The home side had no answer to a marvellous Baggies onslaught which saw them go two goals up in the first six minutes. Albion should have been four up by half time, but in the second half they conceded a penalty, converted by Brady, and had to show extraordinary defensive resilience to hold out in the face of some frenetic attacking by Stapleton, Brady and company — "A second half of the most resolute defence since Mafeking", claimed one national newspaper!

The Tony Brown story is full of great games, most of them, unfortunately restricted to an audience of spectators "at the match". Old Trafford on December 30 1978 was the setting for what is generally acknowledged as one of the greatest games played between two sides in this country in the past twenty or thirty years — and, luckily, the whole game was televised. In the eyes of many pundits, from Atkinson to Clough, Robson to Regis, the game was the footballing high point of the Seventies. few who saw the game, or watched it on ITV, will ever forget it, and many, many Albion fans now have it on video as a reminder of the quality their club could provide, during the dark days in the Second and Third Divisions. To this day, the club still has hundreds of Scandinavia-based supporters who were first enticed to following the club on the basis of that one game, which was transmitted live to viewers in Norway, Denmark and Sweden.

Tony played his full part in what was Albion's last truly great encounter against the Red Devils. There are not enough superlatives to describe the encounter, so we let the facts speak for themselves. Albion were on 29 points, and needed a win to keep in touch with Liverpool (33 points) and Everton (32). Manchester United were in mid-table, having just lost 3-0 at Bolton and 3-0 at home to Liverpool. Albion kicked off on a grey, freezing Manchester afternoon, with snow in the air, facing the Stretford End — and found themselves a goal down after twenty minutes, Greenhoff volleying home a left wing corner.

Six minutes later, Tony equalised, gliding home a low shot on the turn after a subtle dummy from his namesake Alistair. That was followed by a fantastic piledriver from Len Cantello after Cyrille Regis' back-heel had deceived the United defence (and which earned the strike the accolade of *Central TV's* Goal of the Season). United bounced back to level and lead once more. First Gordon McQueen scored with one of his trademark power headers, then Sammy McIlroy ended a mazy dribble through the Albion penalty area with a fine shot past Tony Godden into the top corner — and only 32 minutes gone. Right on the break, Albion drew level once more. Cantello lobbed a ball into the United penalty area and the Bomber won a race with Bryan Robson to nudge the ball over the line for the last goal he would ever score in Manchester!

Three-all at half time, the breathless crowd had ten minutes to recover from the extravaganza of the first period and wait for the thrills that were to follow. Ron Atkinson re-grouped his men at the break, and they exhibited their usual class to dominate the second half completely. With Wile, Batson, Robertson and Statham denying the home side a single chance in the last 45 minutes, Cunningham and Regis ripped open the United defence with further goals on 76 and 83 minutes, Regis only being denied a hat-trick by two superb saves from goalkeeper Gary Bailey. Ron Atkinson reminisced years later. "I've just done a questionnaire for *4-4-2 Magazine*, asking for the three best matches I've ever seen, and I put the Albion 5-3 win at Old Trafford top of the list. Second was England and Germany, for obvious reasons, in the World Cup, and Frankfurt and Real Madrid in the European Cup Final, the 7-3 game at Hampden. But I put a little rider on the form as well — 'Gary Bailey actually kept the score down!'"

As if goals galore and legions of games were not enough for Tony Brown, in that game he achieved a feat which was truly unique — and which might take a thousand games before it happens again — if it ever does. Gary Bailey, the young South

African-born goalkeeper for Manchester United in that epic game was the son of one Roy Bailey; the man who stood between the posts in 1963 when Tony rifled home his first League goal at Portman Road. Tony can claim the unique distinction of scoring League goals past father and son, some fifteen years apart!

That win alone made people sit up and consider Albion for honours. The club were Flavour of the Month even in the *New Musical Express,* who described them as the "In Team" for 1979. Tony was interviewed by the *Sunday Express*. "Tony is now 33 and he recently broke the all time scoring record of that famous Midlands club West Bromwich Albion, and this season joined his hero Denis Law in the exclusive '200 Club' for those rare and gifted craftsmen who have scored a double century of Football League goals. The twilight of his career seems set for a glittering climax. Albion, with their cleverly blended mixture of youth and experience, and the exciting skills of their coloured players, Cunningham, Regis and Batson, are high in the First Division and still in the UEFA Cup. 'I think we can win something this season' says Tony, and coming from him, that's a profound declaration of belief."

As 1978 passed gloriously into footballing history, Albion opened the New Year with a "ballet on ice" against Bristol City at The Hawthorns — a game which went ahead despite a carpet of snow on a rock-hard pitch on a day that saw just three League games survive from a full schedule. Not only was the game on *Match of the Day* — because of the paucity of fixtures, it was the first match ever to be covered live in its entirety on Radio Two that afternoon.

Tony remembers that game not only because of the quality of the Albion's play on the ice, but also because of the way City were "conned" into playing the game on the treacherous surface. "We wore the famous 'pimple boots'. Joe Royle was manager at the time at City and before the game he was in the tunnel with Ron, and he wanted the game called off, 'We can't play on this, it's rubbish!'. Then four or five of us put on the green dimpled boots and ran out on the snow, and they were brilliant, and Ron said, 'Look, they're not having any problems!' Joe said, 'Oh yes, it looks OK' and stopped protesting. But City had the usual leather studs and they couldn't stand up — we murdered them that day! And that was the day when Ally Brown got the daftest booking — for throwing a snowball at the ball just as a City player was taking a penalty!"

The ice and snow that had served Albion so well against City was eventually to cost them very dearly. Temperatures dropped for days on end as snow carpeted all but the south west of the country. Albion's third round trip to Coventry was postponed, but eventually played on

January 9, ending in a thrilling 2-2 draw. Before the replay, Albion travelled to Carrow Road to play Norwich on January 13. The game was in doubt because of the frozen pitch and it seemed that only the vast number of travelling fans, and the presence of the *Match of the Day* cameras swayed the referee's decision. Justin Fashanu made his League debut for Norwich, but it was Cyrille Regis who opened the scoring after just eleven minutes, Norwich relying on an equaliser from World Cup hero Martin Peters after Albion had been reduced to ten men — because Brendan Batson was off the pitch tying up his shoe-laces!

Liverpool's match at home to Aston Villa had fallen victim to the weather, so the draw took Albion to the top of the First Division — for the only time that season. It was also the first time they had topped the entire Football League since winning at Northampton Town more than thirteen years before — and the last time, to date. Of the 22 League games played, they had lost just two, scoring 42 goals and conceding only 20, with a points tally of 34 — one ahead of Liverpool. Tony had played in fifteen of those matches, scoring six goals, which placed him as fourth top scorer at the club behind Ally Brown, Cunningham and Regis.

Albion cruised through into the fourth round of the FA Cup in a 4-0 home win against Coventry City. Tony scored twice in a game that established a new club record of seventeen League and Cup games without defeat, beating the previous record set back at the turn of the century — and Tony had missed only one of those seventeen games, "Cunningham's game", in Valencia.

With Albion — and Tony — very much on the crest of a wave, it seemed as if nothing could stop their relentless charge for the Championship, the FA Cup and the UEFA Cup. Except the weather. As Siberian conditions intensified, Albion were not to play another League game until February 3.

"The weather was so bad that we could only train indoors, and we were desperate to fix up friendlies at places like Portmouth, the Channel Islands and Witney, because round here, you couldn't do anything outside. We just became rusty, and never recovered the way were flying before Christmas. That season, personally, I felt brilliant, fitness-wise and everything, and it was another case of a team coming along when the players complemented each other perfectly. There was tremendous pace in the side, at the back, with Derek Statham, John Wile and Brendan Batson, and up front as well, with Cyrille and Laurie, so we could break with breathtaking speed, and completely destroy teams. A great side; a great time."

Tony's second great Albion side, before the FA Cup semi-final at Highbury in 1978. Back (l-r): George Wright, Paddy Mulligan, Laurie Cunningham, Bryan Robson, Tony Godden, Len Cantello, John Osborne, Alistair Brown, Cyrille Regis, Ron Atkinson. Front row: Derek Statham, John Trewick, Tony Brown, John Wile, Mick Martin, Alistair Robertson, Brendan Batson, Willie Johnston

In between times, Ron Atkinson swooped into the transfer market to break the bank, signing the most expensive uncapped player in the history of the game, £500,000 David Mills — who just couldn't get in the side, setting Atkinson quite a quandary. "I tell you, I'd watched him a lot and I thought he was the ideal replacement for Tony Brown, when Tony eventually packed up — and for Len Cantello as well. He was an England Under-21 and he had been picked for the 1974 full England squad, when Joe Mercer was England manager. Colin Addison actually watched him for fifteen minutes one night at Villa Park, and turned round and said, 'He's the one for me!' And I'd seen him a lot, but... what I should have done, I suppose, was put him straight in the team and say, 'Bugger it!', but the team was going so well in 1979, I didn't want to rock the boat at all..."

Tony was aware that Mills was being lined up as his replacement. "Yes, I knew that Dave Mills was meant to replace me when I'd finished. In the end, I reckon he added two years to my career!"

Albion rolled back into action on Saturday February 3 — but what a venue at which to resume — at a packed Anfield against second placed Liverpool, with an attendance of 52,211 bettered only by the Liverpool Derby game there. At that point, Liverpool had actually lost one more game than the Albion, with defeats at Everton, Arsenal and Bristol, but had only conceded an astonishing nine goals, and had games in hand. In a real thriller, but with Albion noticeably rusty after their long lay-off, goals from Dalglish and Fairclough gave the home side a two goal cushion. Ally Brown pulled a goal back, but near the end, Laurie Cunningham blew Albion's best chance when he elected to shoot instead of laying the ball off to a perfectly placed colleague, and Liverpool stole a crucial lead in the race.

Further postponements of Albion games allowed Liverpool to storm away, and by the time that Albion met Leeds at The Hawthorns three weeks later the Merseysiders were seven points clear at the top. Before the game, much delayed presentations were made to Tony Brown, who received a Capo Di Monte figurine from director Tom Silk, to honour his goals record, and to Ron Atkinson, who had been named *Manager of the Month* for December. February 24th was the first opportunity the club had to stage the presentation, because of the severity of the weather!

Leeds gained some revenge for the Albion's famous win in 1971 by seriously damaging Albion's chances of the Championship, as they won 2-1, despite another Bomber "Special". That was the first game in a series against Leeds which saw the teams meet three times in the space of six days. The following Tuesday, in the fourth round of the FA Cup (played at The Hawthorns because — how familiar — of a ban on FA

Cup games at Elland Road because of crowd violence) the sides drew 3-3 after Albion had thrown away a 3-1 lead in the closing minutes. In the replay, also at the Albion, on the Thursday, the Baggies won through 2-0, after extra time. The hectic schedule continued just two days later with a 1-1 FA Cup draw at home to Southampton, only for the Saints — with the help of a VERY dubious penalty — to win the replay.

Another hat-trick — a proud Tony Brown collects his third Midland Footballer of the Year Award from the former manager of his boyhood heroes: Sir Matt Busby, of Manchester United

Somehow, the side managed to call upon hidden reserves of energy to win the next six games. Tony missed four of those games, against Coventry, Derby, Manchester City and Everton, but he did return for the first leg of Albion's quarter-final tie against Red Star. "The first leg was incredible, with over 100,000 in Belgrade. What an atmosphere — I think somebody got killed there, actually — and we were well pleased with the result, only losing 1-0, but we threw it away by conceding a late goal in the second leg." Indeed they did, as Atkinson regrets to this day. "We should have won the second leg. That was inexperience on the part of all of us, including myself — but all of us were to blame. Savic had scored late on for them out there, with a disputed free-kick. At home, we scored, early doors, well, just before half time, anyway, and we were driving forward at the end to win it. We were THAT much off scoring a goal and they broke on us and the little one —Sestic, was it? — took it out on the right. Ally Robertson, who, two hundred times out of a hundred, would have just stepped across and cleared it, tried to nick it off him, but he took it past Ally and put it in the net. Whereas if we'd said, 'We've got two minutes left, we'll take extra time', then we'd have seen them off in the extra half hour. But that's the sort of team we were, anyway."

Tony didn't return to the side until April 14, when he scored a scrambled goal in a 1-1 draw against Arsenal at The Hawthorns, in what proved to be his last League goal of the season. Albion's form finally began to falter and their title challenge faded away. Tony played in just five of the last ten matches. "I never got back to my pre-Christmas form, personally. But the really sad part about that team was that it broke up so soon. If that could have stopped together for four or five years, it could have done some great things. It came together quickly, and fell apart quickly, but it was a great, top-class side. If I had to choose between the two great sides, 1968 and 1979, I'd have to just go for the latter, because they had more individuals who could change a game — but it would be a close thing."

One last flurry — four wins on the trot, including a very enjoyable 1-0 win at the Villa — meant that Albion went into their last game of the season against third placed Nottingham Forest needing just a draw to secure the runners-up spot which — at least — they had deserved for a marvellous season. Tony returned to the side but Albion managed to shoot themselves in the foot, conceding a goal in the last few minutes to Trevor Francis to lose even that little bit of solace. They finished in third place in Division One for the only time in the club's history. Tony is sanguine about it now. "You never know; we could have won the League that season, although we eventually finished third. Ron always says that that was the best team he has ever managed — and he's managed some good teams. If he had that team now, he'd win it, no problem. But Liverpool were a fantastic side that season, no question; but finishing third was still a fantastic achievement; the best that Albion had managed since 1954."

If Albion failed to pick up any silverware, Tony himself was more fortunate. In a season of presentations to the Bomber, before the game with — appropriately once more — Manchester United, Sir Matt Busby presented Tony with the *Midland Footballer of The Year* award. It was — uniquely — the third time that Tony had collected the accolade, an honour he cherishes to this day.

Not only that, but Tony was also voted joint winner of the Midland Sports Writers *Player of The Year* — along with namesake Ally Brown — and runner-up to Tessa Sanderson in the Variety Club *Sports Personality of the Year*. In early June, the disappointments of the League behind them, Albion travelled away for a three match tour of Denmark, completing it with a 7-0 drubbing over IHF F.C. The last game of a gruelling season, the seventh and final goal was scored by the Bomber.

In the summer of 1979, Len Cantello signed for Bolton, Laurie Cunningham was enticed away by Real Madrid and assistant manager Colin Addison took over as manager of Derby County. The magical '79 side had, in essence, lost three of its vital components, and the club would never again reach such heights as it had in its Centenary Year. Neither would Tony Brown, who was soon to fade from the limelight he had enjoyed for over fifteen years.

One hundred years — and out!

The Baggies started their Centenary season — albeit, as has been discovered since, a year late — with friendlies against a Chine XI, Torquay, Bradford City and Dutch giants Ajax, in the match officially billed as the club's Centenary Game. They won each of those games, without even conceding a goal, before moving on to the final pre-season preparations in Spain. There they lost in a prestigious four club tournament, to Honved and Sporting Gijon, both games ending in 1-0 defeats as Albion finished last. Six games played, and Tony had played in all of them — but, ominously, he had failed to score in any of them.

The Albion's preparations had actually been hit very badly by Cyrille Regis' bad injury against the Chinese, and as a result Atkinson had to reshuffle his attack, which meant that for the opening League game at home to Derby County — managed by Albion's former assistant manager, Colin Addison — Tony wore, unusually, the number nine short in a poor goalless draw. It was a miserable start to a rotten season, Albion failing to record a win until their sixth outing, when the defeated a similarly struggling Manchester City 4-0 at home. They could only score twice in those five games, and only sneaked a 2-1 aggregate win over Fulham in the League Cup.

Boosted by the win over City, Albion travelled to East Germany to meet Carl Zeiss Jena in the UEFA Cup, a match which Atkinson later described as "The worst performance by any team of mine". For Tony Brown, the spell was the worst goal drought of his career, as he failed to score until September 25, when Albion's favourite "bunnies" at that time, Coventry City came to The Hawthorns for a League Cup tie. On this occasion, though, Albion had an early shock when City took a ninth minute lead through Tony English. Wile equalised six minutes later and Tony Brown netted a penalty to win the game.

This was light relief for Tony — subsequently he lost his place in the first team, and was relegated to the bench until October 20, when injuries meant that he was recalled for his 800th first team game — a staggering statistic — in a 4-0 one-sided win against Southampton. The *Albion News* the following week, for the League game against Coventry, recorded the event. "Anyone looking at the Saints game and not knowing the who's who of Albion could have been forgiven if they couldn't believe that the Albion number eleven was taking part in his 800th game for the Baggies. Everyone contributed to a fine team performance, none more so than the young Bomber, who, with a lifetime of soccer behind him, continues to display the courage and artistry of much younger players."

Against Coventry Tony opened his long delayed League goal account for the season. With Albion leading 2-0 and just a few minutes to go, the Baggies were awarded a penalty which Tony converted with his usual aplomb past Les Sealey — his last League penalty for the club, Two minutes later, he slid in an Ally Brown cross from close range to make it 4-0, and on a day of finalities, this was also Tony's last League goal for the Albion. Little did he know it at the time, but Tony had also played in a winning side for the last time. In the next nine games, he played just three times; a 2-1 defeat at Derby, a 1-1 draw with Everton, and another loss at Elland Road.

On January 1 1980, he made his last full appearance for his beloved Albion, ironically enough, at Portman Road, Ipswich, where he had started his professional career as a callow youth some seventeen years before. On that glorious day, he had starred and scored in a 2-1 win — this time he was not so lucky as Ipswich gave Albion a 4-0 thumping in front of 22,000 spectators. Tony's performance did not merit a mention in reports of the game!

Tony was once more relegated to the subs bench for the FA Cup tie at home to West Ham, as Albion fought back against the Second Division side to score an injury time equaliser. In the replay at Upton Park on the following Wednesday, Brown came on as a substitute in the 74th minute, with West Ham leading 1-0. Trevor Brooking, who would, a few months later, score the winning goal for the Hammers against Arsenal in the Cup Final, put his side further ahead, but four minutes from time Tony Brown made sure he went out on a goal-scoring high, at least. The goal came from one of the few clear-cut chances that Albion had created all night, when Peter Barnes crossed from the left for Tony to head home.

The following Saturday, January 12, at Nottingham Forest, Tony played the whole of the second half as a substitute for Peter Barnes. It was his very last outing in a competitive match for the Albion, and was not a happy day. The Baggies led 1-0 at the interval, through a Regis goal, but lost it in the second half as Forest scored three times and sent Albion to fifth from bottom in the First Division — a stark contrast to the heights of the previous season. "The following week I went on as substitute in a League game at Nottingham Forest and that was my final first team game, which I remember most for the fact that Larry Lloyd kicked me in the head and I had concussion for three days after!"

From then on, Tony was left out of the squad completely, being replaced by a new name from the Reserves — little Remi Moses — as the side turned the season around completely to finish in a respectable 11th place. Brown played four Reserve games, scoring twice in a 4-3 win at Bury on March 14.

At the end of the 1979-80 season, a couple of teams from the American NASL enquired to Ron Atkinson about Tony's availability for their summer season. The North American Soccer League had been established in 1967 but had always failed to generate sufficient public support in a country where the triumvirate of American Football, baseball and basketball were king. Then Pele signed for New York Cosmos, and the game took off, and by 1980, there was a well-established network of 24 top professional clubs, split into two Leagues (the National Conference and the American Conference) each divided into three geographical divisions, east, central and west.

Detroit Express, part-owned by Jimmy Hill, playing at the Silverdome in Pontiac, and managed by one-time Watford boss Ken Furphy, were one club keen to sign Tony. They had quite an Albion contingent there, with five players with a one-time connection with the club, Eddie Colquhoun, David Bradford, Jim Holton, Don Nardiello and Gary Bannister all on their roster that year.

They faced strong opposition from two quarters. One was from Tony himself — he just didn't want to uproot himself to spend four or five months in the States! "I really didn't want to go; I just wasn't interested, even though I was obviously coming to the end of my time in the first team at the Albion. Big Ron persuaded me to think about it a bit more. 'Talk to them, and give it a try. Think of it as a holiday'".

So Tony met up with the European scout of the New England Tea Men, Arthur Smith, at the Post House Hotel in Great Barr. Earlier, he had spoken to his old mate Bobby Hope, who had had an enjoyable spell in the States in three seasons with the Philadelphia Atoms and Dallas Tornado. "Bob convinced me that I should give it a try, telling me how good the weather and the lifestyle would be for my family".

So Tony decided to give it a try, and moved his family (wife Irene and three year old son Paul) to Boston Massachusetts for the summer. "In the end, I really enjoyed the experience — but it wasn't a holiday! It was really hard work. It was so hot, and there was so much travelling, all over America. If, say, you played California Surf or Los Angles Aztecs, it meant a trip right across the continent, which was just the same as travelling from England to the States, just to play one game."

The Tea Men played at the Schaefer Stadium, in Foxboro, Mass., a stadium shared with the New England American Football side, who Tony used to marvel at when he had the opportunity to watch some of their violent encounters on his days off. The Tea Men were managed by a former Manchester United man, Irishman Noel Cantwell and, as might be expected perhaps from a New England team, there was a good English connection in the squad. In goal was Kevin Keelan, Norwich City's swarthy Indian-born goalkeeper, plus Jack Carmichael and Chris

Tony, squad number 12, in action for the Tea Men against Edmonton

Turner of Peterborough (Cantwell had also been manager of the Posh for some time), Norman Bell of the Wolves (who was later to have unsuccessful trials at The Hawthorns) and Keith Weller (England, Millwall and Leicester City).

There were plenty of unfamiliar names as well, like Brazilian Renato Cila, and the splendidly named Ringo Cantillo, from Costa Rica, as ell as several home-grown talents, as the NASL clubs tried a mixture of ageing foreign stars and an League-imposed minimum of three Americans, in an attempt to popularise the game with the locals. That minimum would rise to four the following year, and five the year after, and so on, but it failed to have the desired effect, and attendances remained low, as soccer remained the favoured sport only of the families of European immigrants, mostly from Spain and Italy.

There was another English player in the side that Tony remembers well from that period — Bob Newton, a centre-forward who played for a string of clubs including Huddersfield, Hartlepool, Port Vale, Chesterfield and Stockport. "Big Bad Rob we used to call him — the biggest nutter I've ever played with. Ten times worse than Willie Johnston! We were playing New York Cosmos one day, and Franz Beckenbauer was playing for them at the time. We were having the team talk before the game and Noel Cantwell called Big Rob — not one of the brightest of lads — over for a chat. 'Beckenbauer will probably be marking you', Noel said. 'Watch out for him, because he's a good player'. 'Who?' 'Franz Beckenbauer, the famous German International'. He'd never heard of him, but he was game. 'German? Ah... leave him to me!' We'd only been playing five minutes. The ball went in between the two of them and Rob went right over the top on Beckenbauer — nearly snapped him in two, and he was rolling over and over on the floor in agony. Rob went over to him, leaned over and said, 'German bastard!' As the referee came over, I thought, Oh dear, Bob! And off he went!"

That was not Newton's only brush with authority. "Bob did the Fort Lauderdale's Chilean international centre-half, with his elbow, opened up all his face; it was a terrible injury. Fort Lauderdale were suing the club for millions, and Bob personally for a million dollars because of it. But Bob said, 'They'll have a job getting a million out of me — I've only got ten quid back at home in the bank in Hartlepool!'"

Tony, still contracted to the Albion, of course, arrived a few weeks late for the start of the American season, but only missed the opening game of their 32 game season, away to Atlanta on April 5 1980. He made his NASL debut a week later, ironically enough against the other American side that he had rejected, Detroit Express, at the Pontiac

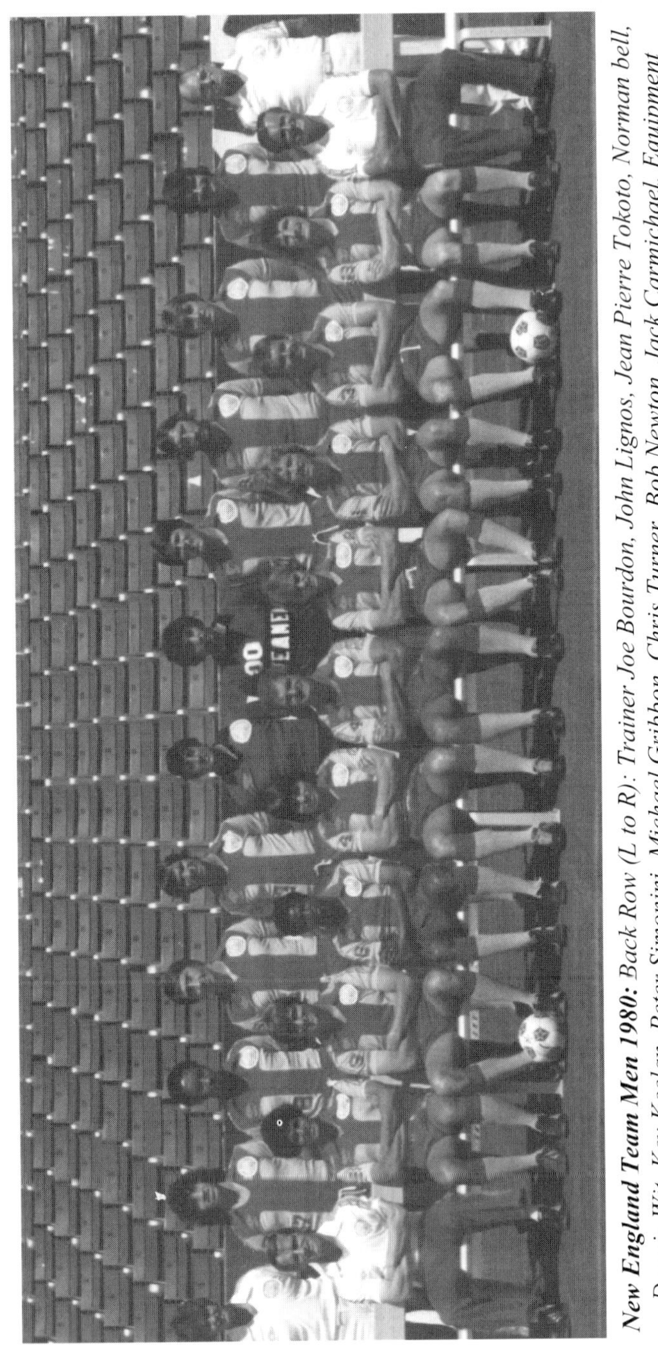

New England Team Men 1980: *Back Row (L to R): Trainer Joe Bourdon, John Lignos, Jean Pierre Tokoto, Norman bell, Dennis Wit, Kev Keelan, Peter Simonini, Michael Gribbon, Chris Turner, Bob Newton, Jack Carmichael, Equipment Manager Dick Hobbs. Front row (L to R): Assistant coach Dennis Violett, Juan Cano, Garnett Moen, Keita, Ringo Cantillo, Keith Weller, Artur, Kevin Walsh, Peter Carr,* ***Tony Brown****, Head Coach Noel Cantwell.*

Silverdome in front of a meagre 10,000 crowd, starting off his US career with a 1-0 defeat.

It took Tony some time to settle in to the new style of football. "It was a bit strange — it was all new at the time, we played the same rules for offside, almost, as we had done in the Watney Cup experiment back in 1971, except we had a 35 yard line out from goal — you could only be offside beyond that line — nowhere else. There were shoot-outs, and overtime; I tell you, it didn't half open the game up, and I know you might say that it was only American football, but there were some very good players over there. The game was far more entertaining. And the pay was good — more than I was getting at the Albion at the time."

It took Tony fifteen games to get onto the scoresheet — after being relegated to the subs' bench a couple of times — but he hit his first NASL goal at home to Minnesota in a 3-2 win at home on June 21.

Goals came a lot easier after that, and once Tony got back into the swing of it, he hit six in seven games, ending the season as third top scorer behind Bob Newton and Malian international Salif Keita, with eight goals (and fourteen "assists") in his 28 starts.

With a League system of six points for a win plus one point per goal up to a maximum of three (with fifteen minute sudden-death overtime in the case of a tie after 90 minutes, and a 35 yard shoot out after that), the Tea Men qualified for the end of season Play-offs by virtue of beating Tampa Bay Rowdies 1-0 in their last regular season game. Unfortunately, five days later, the Rowdies engineered an early return home for Tony by winning home and away in the first round of the knock-out for the Soccer Bowl.

That last League game against Tampa Bay had attracted the second biggest gate of the season to the Schaefer Stadium — 25,132 — a figure only bettered, home and away, by the two games against the top side in the NASL, New York Cosmos, who went on to beat Fort Lauderdale in the Soccer Bowl Final at the end of September. But by then, Tony was back in England, well into his twentieth season with West Bromwich Albion.

He made his first Central League appearance of the new season at home to Sheffield United on September 17, and the *Express & Star* made a point of recording his return to English football. "Albion's favourite son returned to The Hawthorns last night after his summer-long exile. And the experienced marksman nearly celebrated with a goal. It was vintage Brown, as he turned to hoist a right foot shot over his shoulder and into the net — but a linesman's flag ruled him offside!" Albion still won the match 1-0, with a goal from Nicky Cross.

A week earlier, Tony had made a first team appearance when the side jetted out to Naples to draw 2-2 in a friendly with Napoli, in front of a big crowd that had turned out to see new signing Rudi Krol's (who, coincidentally, applied for the Albion manager's job after Ray Harford resigned in 1997) first game for the Italians, and that was to be Tony's role for the '80-81 season — flitting between the Reserves and first team friendlies and testimonial games. All told he managed 13 Reserve games, scoring twice, with his final goal at The Hawthorns coming in a 4-0 Central League win over Blackpool on October 1 1981 — from a classic 25 yard trademark free kick! His last Reserve team game on the ground came on Saturday January 24 1981, in a 2-1 win over Burnley; a month before, Pearce, the young goalkeeper of Blackburn Rovers, laid claim to saving the last penalty that Tony ever took for the club.

For the first team, on less serious business, Tony played against Norwich at Spalding in a testimonial on October 13. On Monday December 8, he was a second half sub at Underhill as Albion beat non-League Barnet 5-0 — and he netted the fifth goal, his final effort for the Albion first team. On Monday February 2, he played his last first team game at The Hawthorns — but only 3,217 fans were there to see it, as Albion defeated Red Star Belgrade 4-2 in a friendly — as Tony came on for Gary Owen for the last 27 minutes of the game. His very last game in a first team shirt was in a match played at Poole Town, to celebrate the southern side's Centenary. Albion won 4-2 and Tony did not come back out after the interval, so we can safely say that sometime around 7.45 pm on February 23 1981, The Bomber's first team career with the Albion came to a close.

Tony knew his time was up at the top. "The balls that you used to get on the end of, you just didn't get to any more. I just wanted to stop at the Albion as long as I could. I had a three year contract, and Ron wanted me to play in the Reserves. Also, I'd been promised a Testimonial game. I'd had one after ten years at the Albion, and Ron promised me another at the end of my contract, which marked twenty years service. Ron said to me, 'You're still in the squad, and you could be in if we get any injuries' — he wanted me to see my time out at the club, which was great of him. I was still enjoying it, still involved. I knew my time was up, but I was looking forward to my Testimonial. By the summer of 1981, I had hardly played any football at all. A few games in the Reserves, a few friendlies, although Ron had always kept me involved with the first team, making sure I always travelled away with them. At the end of that season, Ron told me about an offer to play in America again, but that the Tea Men had moved from Boston to Jacksonville, in Florida. I jumped at it this time, and out to the States the three of us went again."

The NASL clubs were all owned by large conglomerates — the Tea Men, not surprisingly, owned by Lipton's Tea Inc. — and if they felt that they were not getting the crowds that they needed, they would up sticks and transfer the franchise hundreds or even thousands or miles across the country to another state.

So the New England Tea Men — neat name, coming from Boston — became the Jacksonville Tea Men, still managed by Noel Cantwell, but playing at the Gator Bowl, Jacksonville, near the Gulf of Mexico

Some of the players were the same. Tony, of course, retaining his number twelve squad number from the year before, and Newton, Cantillo and Carmichael, plus a smattering of new faces, including Coventry's Alan Green, Wolves' Colin Brazier, Yugoslavian Nino Zec and Argentinean star Jorge Berrio.

A big benefit of the move for Tony was that his "new" team played on real grass, instead of the Astroturf that he had hated so much in Boston. Otherwise, things were very much the same. "The weather, the lifestyle was great. It was lovely for the family; there seemed to be barbecues every day in the sunshine, they gave you a car, a luxury apartment — all you had to find was your food and your petrol. And we were playing with some big names again, like Beckenbauer, Neeskens, Cruyff, and the NASL game was really taking off. The highlight of those two years for me was playing against Johann Cruyff, who really turned it on in one game against the Tea Men. Like Besty had done in that 7-0 defeat at United in 1970, he'd been electric, even though he was 33 and near the end of his career — it was an honour just to be on the same pitch."

In fact, that season marked the start of the decline of the NASL which was to see the end of big-time professional soccer in the States by 1984, when the League went bankrupt. In 1981, the number of teams dropped to twenty as Atlanta, Houston, Memphis, Rochester — and Detroit — all folded, but the fixture computer still managed to organise a 32 match season for the remaining clubs.

This time Tony was able to leave England in good time, and made his "debut" for Jacksonville in the opening game of the season on March 28 at home to Toronto, Alan Green scoring on HIS debut to give the Tea Men a 1-0 win. It took Tony eight games to get of the mark, scoring the Tea Men's goal in a 2-1 defeat (after a shoot-out) in Fort Lauderdale on May 1. Tony hated the shoot-out system of determining matches. "You had to run for goal from the 35 yard line that they used for offside, and you had five seconds to get your shot in before the whistle blew. I didn't like it at all, especially on Astroturf, because the best way of taking them was to lift the ball into the air as you started your run, so you could lift it over the keeper as he came out — but you couldn't get your foot under the ball on Astroturf. I hated it. I scored one and missed two of the three I had to take."

Once again, after a slow start, the goals began to flow, and Tony scored two in a 4-0 win over California a few weeks later, his best single game return in his two years in the States. He played against several names familiar to Albion supporters, including Willie Johnston and Bruce Grobbelaar at Vancouver, where Johnny Giles was coach and Alan Merrick, who now runs a soccer coaching academy in America, against San Jose.

Tony played in every game that season, scoring nine goals and finishing as second top scorer behind Green, although his ten assists made him the club's top goal provider for the second season running — perhaps some of Don Howe's training had come home to roost after all!

Once again, Tony reached the Play-offs, and fared a little better, beating Atlanta in the first round at home and away before losing in a third game decider at San Diego on September 9, leaving Tony free to return to The Hawthorns for his 21st season. Tony failed to score in his five Play-off games, so the last goal that he scored in American football was witnessed by just 5,748 spectators in a 5-0 end of season win at Edmonton on August 19. There was to be no third season for Tony's family in America — "I wasn't asked!" — and Jacksonville finished bottom of the Southern Division in 1983, disappearing into oblivion shortly afterwards.

In the Fourth Division, Tony gets in a header for Torquay against Colchester

Back in West Bromwich, events had occurred which were to end Tony's association with West Bromwich Albion. That summer, Ron Atkinson had taken the Albion out on an American West Coast Tour, in which they had met Edmonton Drillers, Vancouver Whitecaps and Seattle Sounders, ending with a break in Fort Lauderdale Ron Atkinson takes up the story. "I went into this bar and Frank Worthington strolled in. He'd been playing for Tampa Bay Rowdies against Fort Lauderdale and he came into the bar where we all were. He said to me, 'You're the next United manager. I'm telling you — I know. Lawrie McMenemy's turned it down'. I went to Paris to watch the European Cup Final shortly afterwards and when I was there, I got a phone call from a guy I didn't know, who asked me if I'd be interested in the United job, and immediately, I said, 'Well, I'd have to be interested — what's it about?' And he told me that when I landed in Manchester from Paris, somebody would be meeting me at the airport. And he met me at the airport, took me to a house — and that was it."

It certainly was. Ron Atkinson had been lured away from the Albion by Manchester United — a move which was to have disastrous consequences for Tony Brown. When he got back to England, Ronnie Allen was back at the helm. Tony, revitalised by his second trip to the States, was looking forward to possibly winning back a place in the first team under the "new" man, who, of course, had managed him with the Albion for six short months in 1977. It was not to be.

"I went into Allen's office, and when he asked me my plans, I told him I had a year of my contract left, and I wanted to see that out and arrange the Testimonial that had been promised me by Ron, and the club, to mark twenty years as an Albion player. The manager told me straight away that he wanted me out of the club quickly as possible, and that there were two or three clubs in the lower division who were interested. I told him I didn't want to go, and refused to talk to anybody, but he made it really difficult for me, making me train with the kids, having me back in the afternoons and refusing to get me involved at all. So in the end, I had enough. I didn't want to be treated like that at my age, so I agreed to talk to other clubs.

Tony played just one more game in an Albion shirt that season; his last in a twenty one year association with the club. It was for the Reserves, at Bloomfield Road on Wednesday August 23 1981, when he wore the number eleven jersey in the following line-up: *Grew, Conniff, Cowdrill, Lowery, Ebanks, Danks, Monaghan, Lewis, Summerfield, Benjamin (Sub: Luke), Brown* — and just 196 people were there to see Blackpool Reserves win 2-0.

The two clubs interested in signing Tony were Port Vale, managed by John McGrath, and Torquay, led by Frank O'Farrell, another Manchester United name from the past. The big factor in Tony's decision to sign to play on the "English Riviera" was not the weather, or the beaches — but one Gary Pendrey. Signed by Ron Atkinson from Birmingham City in 1979, as cover for the oft-injured Derek Statham, Pendrey soon developed a strong friendship with Tony at the Albion. He signed for Torquay in August 1981, and it was on his recommendation — and after the two decided to share the cost and hassle of driving down from the Midlands together for matches — that Tony decided to make the big break.

"I had a chat with Frank O'Farrell then went to Ronnie Allen and told him the news. Knowing that I intended to carry on living in Walsall, I didn't ask Allen if I could train with the Albion, only if I could use their facilities. 'No way'. No explanation, and I still don't know to this day why he refused such a simple request, unless he thought I was some sort of threat to him at the club. I remember that in his first spell as manager, he had made all sorts of little remarks, about how he was going to drop me before I beat his Albion scoring record, and I used to wonder, 'Is he serious?', because you never knew with Ronnie".

Anyway, I was in the portakabins on the site where they were building the new Halfords Lane stand, discussing the move with Frank, and in walked Ronnie. He went over to Frank, and said 'Look after him — he's a good lad, he is'. And I thought — 'Bloody hell!' And after all that service, they — I don't know who set the amount — also insisted on a £6,000 fee, so they STILL made a profit on me!"

Somehow — not from Tony — news of Ronnie Allen's uncharitable behaviour got into the local press, and caused quite an outcry, with Allen going as far as banning all his players from talking to the press again without his permission. Jim Smith, manager at Birmingham City, got to hear about it, and offered the opportunity to train at Blues, which he gratefully took up.

"I should never have left the Albion in the circumstances that I did. If I could have just stopped until the end of my contract, that last season. fixed a Testimonial game up and then left, it would have been grand, and everybody would have been happy. It wasn't right to end my time at the club like that, after so many happy years at a club I loved."

Brown's first game in the unfamiliar white shirt and blue shorts of the Gulls was at Plainmoor on Saturday October 17 1981, wearing the number four shirt in a 2-1 defeat by Tranmere Rovers. Three games later, and Gary Pendrey was gone, after an altercation with the management, and Tony was left to make the tedious journey down to the south-west by himself. Later in the season, Pendrey got himself fixed up as assistant manager to Alan Buckley at Walsall, and the later, given the nod by Pendrey, generously offered Tony training facilities at Fellows Park, just round the corner from Tony's Walsall home.

After a rough start at Plainmoor, with the crowd getting on his back because of their great expectations from a First Division player, Tony found his feet and started to do what he was still best at — scoring goals, and ended the season as Torquay's top scorer with 11 goals as the club finished in 15th place in Division Four.

Despite his belated success, Tony never really enjoyed his spell in the Fourth Division. "It was a different world altogether, playing for Torquay after so long at the Albion. The biggest difference were the grounds, and the first games I played after leaving the First Division behind were at Hartlepool, Halifax and Rochdale. It was a real eye-opener, just going into the dressing rooms! I'd played all my career at the top, more or less, and it was quite a shock. When they asked me to stop for the following season, I told them I didn't want it, not least because the travelling was just getting too much. They kept ringing me up and persuaded me to sign for another season, but I didn't enjoy it, didn't score any goals, and the whole thing became too much of a chore."

Tony made only four full appearances in 1982-83 before he decided to call it a day. His last game in the Football League came at Port Vale on December 28 1982, when the Gulls were beaten 1-0 by a side led at centre-forward by a face familiar to Tony — Bob Newton, the New England "nutter"!

It was Tony's 619th appearance in the Football League, in a professional career spanning nineteen years. He had scored 229 goals in the League, had never been sent off and had only been booked on two or three occasions in a competition that he had graced. What a shame that he couldn't have gone out with a win.

Tony, and his new manager at Torquay, Bruce Rioch, agreed that he could leave the club "by mutual consent" and Tony looked for part-time football nearer home. Colin Clarke, manager of Alliance Premier (now the Football Conference) side Stafford Rangers a pal of Ron Atkinson from their Oxford days together, had been given the wink by Big Ron and he rang up Tony offering him a contract.

Tony's first game for Stafford was in a 4-0 defeat at Altrincham on February 19 1983. A week later, he played his first game at Marston Road, and proved that he was still not finished as a goal scoring force by notching a goal on his home debut, a 1-1 draw against Kettering. That was followed by another 1-1 draw at Boston United, and then a 1-0 home defeat by Runcorn before Tony scored again — just sixty seconds after the kick off — in a 2-1 home win over Wealdstone, on March 15.

Tony's final goal in senior football — inevitably, from the penalty spot — came for Stafford on March 26, in another 1-1 draw, at home to Bangor City. By now, Stafford had slipped into bottom spot in the Alliance, although the side did well to achieve a 3-3 draw against Crewe at Gresty Road on April 12, which was Tony's last appearance on a Football League ground.

On Thursday, April 21, Tony had had enough, and he bowed out of professional football for good. "I decided to give it a try at Stafford, but I only played a handful of games, and scored just two or three goals. I wasn't enjoying it, and I'd always promised myself that as soon as I stopped enjoying playing the game, I'd give it up. That's why I can remember my last paid game as a semi-professional. It was at Telford. We'd lost 2-0, and after the game I told Colin I was retiring from the game, and that was it, I was finished with football." Colin Clarke told the local paper how sad he was at Tony's decision. "There won't be a better professional or a nicer guy at Stafford. In truth, Tony probably knew we could not afford him next season" — wise words, as Stafford dropped out of the Alliance League into regional football.

Tony's strongest memory about his time at Stafford was unconnected with football — it was a "near death experience!" "I remember once incident very vividly about my time at Stafford. I was coming back home to Walsall after training, down the Broadway, and I'd just stopped at the chip shop, and was eating some chips, when I just clipped the kerb. I turned the car over, and the next thing, I was sailing down the Broadway upside down. Everything flashed before me — 'I'm going to be dead here!' — but the car stopped, and people came to help me out, and force the doors open. They took me into the house, got me a cup of tea and the police came and I was breathalysed, which was OK, and everything. Then they gave me the telephone, so I could ring my wife. 'Hello, I've crashed the car, turned it upside down on the Broadway' 'How did you do that? 'Well, I was eating these chips, and turned round to get one, and clipped the kerb' 'Didn't you get me any chips — Oh, you like looking after yourself, don't you!' I couldn't believe it!"

After leaving Stafford, Tony worked full-time as a sales representative for an electrical wholesalers in West Bromwich — a job he had been preparing for alongside his part-time football at Marston Road. But the lure of football was too great. On February 14 1984, Johnny Giles returned to The Hawthorns as the new manager, replacing Ron Wylie and bringing along his 'A Team' of Nobby Stiles and Norman Hunter, as coaches. Not long after his appointment, Tony got a phonecall from the Irishman. "John asked me to take the schoolboy training at the Albion, and I jumped at it. I did it until Norman Hunter left to become manager at Rotherham in June 1985, which was when John invited me to move onto the full-time coaching staff at the club".

Tony was coaching several youngsters who went on to football fame after leaving the Albion, including David Burrows (Liverpool and Coventry), Carlton Palmer (Leeds and Southampton), Andy Thompson (Wolves), Wayne Dobbins and Mark Robinson (Swindon).

Another, older player who used to enthusiastically join the youngsters for five-a-side games in the cramped Spring Road gym was Steve Bull. "Steve used to blast in shots from all angles into those little five-a-side goals. I thought he was a good lad, raw as anything even though his control wasn't brilliant. He reminded me very much of the way Lee Hughes is now; put defenders under pressure and score lots of goals. I like goalscorers, because that was my forte; I liked Bully and I would have kept him."

With the first team, Tony had no title other than coach, very much in the role that Cyrille Regis has now, attending with the first team and backing up Giles, who still insisted in carrying out virtually all of the first team coaching duties himself.

Tony had been in position for just a matter of months when Giles left the club once more. "I don't like to use it as an excuse, but the injury list was horrific at the start of the '85-86 season. He could hardly put a team out sometimes, and the results were awful, and there were other problems. John was his own man, as always, and

From one generation to another — Tony, now coach at the Albion, in 1985, tells 18 year old David Burrows that he's in the first team squad

he resigned after a defeat at Coventry at the end of September." Nobby Stiles took over as caretaker manager, and with a slight improvement in results, agreed to hold onto the job for a while, until Ron Saunders was appointed in February 1986 — deliberately brought in to do a "clearing out" of the high-paid big name players — and Tony was also on borrowed time.

"It was a horrible time. His philosophy on football, he told us when he arrived, was to get the biggest centre-forward that he could get, and just welly balls up at him, and the rest of the team would have to play off him!" Saunders set upon his new role with relish, getting rid of Tony Godden, Ally Robertson, Imre Varadi, Mickey Thomas, Tony Grealish, Steve Hunt and, eventually, Garth Crooks, Steve MacKenzie, Steve Bull, Andy Thompson, Robbie Dennison and Derek Statham — a whole team of top-rated talent, in the right hands. "Ron used to tell me to take the senior players that he didn't want involved, like Ally and Tony and Mickey and run them into the ground, separate from the other players. I just couldn't do it, so we ended up with a five-a-side game — but what can you do?"

At the end of the season, Tony's second spell at the club was ended and he slipped quietly from The Hawthorms. There was no fuss — Tony just faded off the scene, and returned to his job as a sales rep, until, once again, he got a phonecall out of the blue. "Garry Pendrey had been assistant manager at Wolves after leaving Walsall, and in May 1987 he was given the job as manager of Birmingham City, and he asked me if I wanted to go on the coaching staff at St Andrews. And I said yes."

It many ways, though, it was out of the frying pan and into the fire. After a disappointing season at the Albion, it was, if anything, even worse at the Blues. "They were desperate days. They had no money, nowhere to train, nothing. Ken Wheldon had bought the club for nothing, and he told Garry to sell any half decent players he had to raise cash. I felt really sorry for Garry. He sold Steve Wigley, Julian Dicks, Steve Whitton, all good players. Because we had no money, Garry and I concentrated a lot on the youth set-up there and brought a few good kids through, like Tait, Sturridge and a few others who did well.".

So how did Tony feel when he returned to The Hawthorns on February 25 1989, as coach with Birmingham City for a game that was crucial to both sides, with Albion looking for promotion to Division One and Birmingham hoping to avoid a first-ever relegation to Division Three? "It was a funny experience, sitting there on the away bench. You've been there twenty years, against your old team, against the blue and white stripes. It brought all the old memories flooding back. But you've got to be professional about it." And Tony went out of The Hawthorns with his head held high, as his struggling Blues side managed to grab a goalless draw. At the end of that season, Albion failed to go up, but Blues went down, the Kumars came in and Garry Pendrey was out. Before that, Tony had decided he had enough, and finally terminated his connection with the professional game.

Tony had finished with football — almost, but not quite. He continued to play for the Albion Old Stars side. "Yes, I loved playing for the Old Stars on a Sunday. I really used to look forward to those games on a Sunday morning. The team was run by a lad called Jeff Snape, and we had people like Bobby Hope, Gary Pendrey, Campbell Crawford, John Wile, Johnny Giles, Brendan Batson, Stan Jones and Graham Lovett."

But eventually, even that footballing relaxation had to end. In his final year in America, Tony had begun to be troubled by a painful hip condition, a legacy, he believes, of years of cortisone injections, accentuated by playing on Astroturf surfaces in the NASL. The condition continued to deteriorate and two years after he had finished playing, it had got so bad that he had to have an artificial hip joint fitted — with his other hip also starting to cause him a lot of pain as well. "The worst thing was, I had to give up playing for the All Stars, which is what I missed most. I'd always been fit, I'd always run every day — and all that was gone once I had the hip done."

Now his sole interest in football is watching the club that he spent twenty glorious years with. He attends all the games at The Hawthorns — the club have named a bar after him in the Halfords Lane Stand — and manages to get to many of the away games as well, and is looking forward to the possibility of the club returning to the top flight under manager Denis Smith in 1999.

Tony had no regrets about any of his time at the Albion — none whatsoever, even during the dark days of the mid-Seventies. "The twenty years I was at the club were brilliant; even the bad spells under Don Howe. I don't think I'd change it if I could. It was absolutely brilliant, and I was doing something I really enjoyed. The fans were really brilliant with me at the Albion; absolutely superb. They used to give

Yes, it's Jeff Astle and Tony Brown, once feared by defenders throughout the land, on stage in Jeff's Roadshow in 1998...

you such a lift. Goalscorers are lucky because they get all the praise and supporters like them more than any other players because of the goals. They chanted my name for years; obviously you get stick when you're not playing well, but they were always tremendous to me, and they still are, whenever I go to the Supporters Clubs nowadays."

And he is appreciative of the honours he gained with the club. "I had a lot of success with the Albion really, winning an FA Cup winners medal, a League Cup winners medal, as well as a runners-up medal in the League Cup, and my international cap. One of the things I'm really proud of is winning the *Midlands Player of The Year* Award three times — nobody else ever managed that, and I'm proud of that, and one of the biggest thrills of my career, apart from the cap and the Finals, was receiving my third award from Sir Matt Busby, because, for me, as an old supporter of United, he was 'the one' — the best manager ever, I think."

I was never sent off during my career, and only booked three or four times. My favourite games? Oldham, of course, and the West Ham League Cup Final, which was our best performance, but the Oldham match has to rank alongside that. The Oldham game was so important — but if it had been an ordinary game, won 1-0, nobody would have remembered it. But we had so many exciting games, like the 5-3 at United, but we also beat United and Spurs in some great games, 4-3, 3-3, 5-4 — some fantastic matches. Every time I scored against Manchester United it gave me a lot of satisfaction, after supporting the Busby Babes side as a kid." At heart, though, Tony will be happy to be remembered for his goals at the Albion — a record that almost certainly will never be beaten.

"Of all the records I set at the Albion, it was the one for most goals that was the best. As a goalscorer, for me, that was what the game was all about — scoring goals. If I wasn't scoring, I don't think I was doing my job. That was what I was there for, and that was the greatest thrill that anybody could hope to have, to be honest — scoring goals.

Tony's all-time team of players he has played against during his career.

Banks; Carlos Alberto, Mike England, Franz Beckenbauer, Ray Wilson; Johann Cruyff, Bobby Charlton, Helmut Haller, George Best, Jimmy Greaves, Denis Law

Tony's all-time team of Albion players he has played alongside

John Osborne; Brendan Batson, Wile, Robertson, Derek Statham; Johnny Giles, Bobby Hope, Bryan Robson; Jeff Astle, Cyrille Regis, Willie Johnston Subs: Clive Clark, Laurie Cunningham, Asa Hartford, John Kaye, Graham Lovett

Don't say Brown — say goals!

Tony Brown scored 306 first class goals in a fabulous playing career with three clubs; Albion, Torquay and the New England/Jacksonville Team Men. He scored another 34 goals in various friendlies, tour and testimonial games, and we list them all here (first class goals numbered sequentially, in bold), with a one line description of ALL his League and Cup goals for the Baggies. We also include the time that each of those Albion goals were scored, and the other scorers in each game.

1963-64

1. September 28 1963 **Ipswich Town 1 Albion 2** Division One (*Brown, Clark*)
21 minutes: Brown ran onto a Fraser pass, dribbled past two defenders on the by-line to score with a fine rising shot into the roof of the net.
2. October 12 1963 **Albion 4 Aston Villa 3** Division One (*Brown, Cram, Jackson, Foggo*)
71 minutes: Simpson's dazzling right wing run ended with a sharp low cross that young Tony Brown slid in from six yards.
3. February 1 1964 **Burnley 3 Albion 2** Division One (*Brown, Clark)*
44 minutes: From an astute Kaye pass, Brown swept the ball past Blacklaw into the net.
4. April 11 1964: **Albion 2 Nottingham Forest 3** Division One (*Brown, Foggo*)
28 minutes: Foggo's cross was headed down across goal by Clark and Brown doubled himself up to head past Grummitt.
5. April 18 1964 **Sheffield United 2 Albion 1** Division One (*Brown*)
Brown beat the offside trap from Fenton's pass and calmly placed the ball past Hodgkinson, with all the United defence appealing.

1964-65

August 12 1964 **ADO Den Haag 1 Albion 2** Pre-season Tour (*Brown, Fraser*)
6. August 22 1964 **Manchester United 2 Albion 2** Division One (*Brown, Foulkes og*)
13 minutes: From a Foggo centre, Brown side-footed the ball well wide of Gaskell in the United goal
7/8/9. August 26 1964 **Albion 4 Sunderland 1** Division One (*Brown 3, Clark*)
41 minutes: Brown slammed the ball past 15 year old Forster in the Sunderland goal after Kaye had hit the bar.
64 minutes: Foggo beat the Sunderland defence to cross and Brown tapped in past a bemused keeper.
89 minutes: In a repeat of the second goal, Brown completed his first Albion hat-trick with a simple close range tap-in.
10. September 2 1964 **Sunderland 2 Albion 2** Division One (*Brown, Clark*)
1 minute: A close range shot from a low Foggo cross stunned a 50,000 Roker Park crowd.
11. September 12 1964 **Albion 5 Stoke City 3** Division One (*Cram 3, Foggo, Brown*)
70 minutes: Following a clever lob from Bobby Hope, Brown lobbed a header over the keeper for the fifth goal.
12. November 14 1964 **Blackburn 4 Albion 2** Division One (*Fraser, Brown*)
50 minutes: Brown drove Clark's cross low past Else to put Albion 2-1 ahead at Ewood Park.
13/14. April 19 1964 **Albion 4 West Ham United 2** Division One (*Brown 2, Foggo, Astle*)
24 minutes: When Ray Crawford crossed from the right, Brown beat his namesake in the West Ham goal from close range. The first time Brown and Astle figured on the score-sheet together.
58 minutes: Brown miskicked with his left foot at Fraser's cross, but the ball fell to his right, which made no mistake.
April 28 1964 **Albion 4 Albion Past XI 6** G Williams Testimonial (*Brown, Cram, Kaye, Crawford*)

1965-66

15. September 7 1965 **Everton 2 Albion 3** Division One (*Brown, Astle, Kaye*)
15 minutes: Kaye headed down Williams' cross from the left for Brown to score with a superb half-volley

16. September 18 1965: **Albion 6 Stoke City 2** Division One (*Kaye 3, Brown, Cram, Setters og*)
49 minutes: Astle slipped the ball inside to Brown, who scored with a low angled shot.
17/18. September 22 1965 **Albion 3 Walsall 1** League Cup (*Brown 2, Bennett og*)
42 minutes: The defenders covering Astle missed Brown, drifting in, to score with a beautifully taken shot.
83 minutes: Tucked home a good low cross from Clark to seal Albion's first-ever win in the League Cup
19/20. October 9 1965 **Albion 4 Sunderland 1** Division One (*Brown 2, Kaye, Cram*)
62 minutes: After Montgomery saved Clark's effort, Brown stooped to head in the rebound from five yards.
67 minutes: Another header, from a perfect left wing Astle cross.
21. October 13: **Leeds United 2 Albion 4** League Cup (*Brown, Astle, Kaye, Clark*)
7 minutes: An Astle pass, ended with a close range header from Brown.
22. October 23: **Albion 3 Liverpool 0** Division One (*Brown, Kaye, Clark*)
26 minutes: A pin-point Clark centre finished off with a cross-shot past Lawrence into the corner.
23/24. November 6 1965 **Albion 6 Fulham 2** Division One (*Brown 2, Lovett 2, Wilson, Clark*)
47 minutes: Brown ran past two defenders onto a long Hope pass to shoot into the top corner.
68 minutes: Played on-side by a defender, Brown beat Macedo in a one on one from Kaye's pass.
25. November 10 1965 **Albion 6 Coventry City 1** League Cup (*Astle 3, Fraser 2, Brown*)
40 minutes: Clark fed Kaye, who turned the ball on for Brown to score with a close range blast.
26. November 13 1965 **Blackpool 1 Albion 1** Division One (*Brown*)
58 minutes: Brown put the ball in the net at the second attempt from a great Clive Clark pass.
27. November 17 1965 **Albion 3 Aston Villa 1** League Cup (*Kaye 2, Brown*)
14 minutes: After Govan saved brilliantly from Astle's volley, Brown nipped in for the rebound.
28. November 20 1965 **Albion 2 Blackburn Rovers 1** Division One (*Brown, Cram*)
57 minutes: From a by-line cross from Clark, Brown ran in to volley past a well-beaten Else.
29. December 1 1965 **Albion 2 Peterborough United 1** League Cup semi-final (*Brown, Astle*)
22 minutes: A sharp header over the out-rushing Duff from a Clark cross, to bring Albion level.
30. December 4 1965 **Albion 1 Sheffield United 1** Division One (Brown)
20 minutes: From a fast low Clark cross, Brown hit a shot into the net which never left the ground.
31/32/33. December 15 1965 **Peterborough 2 Albion 4** League Cup semi-final (*Brown 3, Crawford*)
18 minutes: Ray Crawford headed down a Kaye cross for Brown to score from close range.
57 minutes: A superb shot from a defence splitting Hope pass.
85 minutes: Clark beat a string of defenders to unselfishly lay on a tap-in for Brown's first cup hat-trick
34/35. January 1 1966 **Sunderland 1 Albion 5** Division One (*Brown 2, Kaye, Hope, Crawford)*
57 minutes: Another beautiful Clark cross fired home from close range.
76 minutes: Brown chested down a free kick, swivelled and scored with a well-placed shot on the turn.
36. January 15 1966 **Liverpool 2 Albion 2** Division One (*Brown, Kaye*)
11 minutes: Losing the defence, Brown scored with a cross-shot from 20 yards that went in off thepost.
37. February 5 1966 **Albion 5 Nottingham Forest 3** Division One (*Brown, Clark, Kaye, Hope, Cram*)
65 minutes: Kaye pulled the ball back from the by-line, Foggo dummied and Brown scored from close range.
38. February 11 1966 **Albion 2 Aston Villa 2** Division One (*Brown, Kaye*)
68 minutes: Brown headed Albion in front from a delicate Hope chip.
39. March 19 1966 **Albion 1 Burnley 2** Division One (*Brown*)
24 minutes: A Williams long ball headed on by Lovett for Brown to hammer a right foot shot past Blacklaw.
40. February 23 1966 **Albion 4 West Ham United 1** League Cup Final (*Brown, Clark, Williams, Kaye*)
19 minutes: Long through ball, and a lob over the stranded Standen, Clark making sure on the goal line.
41. April 9 1966 **Albion 2 Blackpool 1** Division One (*Brown, Foggo*)
82 minutes: Brown blasted home a late equaliser from a Foggo corner.
May 13 1966 **Alianza Lima 2 Albion 3** End of season tour (*Brown 2, Cram*)
May 15 1966 **Sporting Cristal 1 Albion 2** End of season tour (*Brown, Kaye*)

1966-67

42. August 31 1966 **Albion 2 Leeds United 0** Division One (*Brown, Clark*)
51 minutes: Astle headed down a Hope cross for Brown to score with a header.
43. September 3 1966 **Nottingham Forest 2 Albion 1** Division One (*Brown*)
21 minutes: From a Hope corner, Brown darted in to score with the inside of his right foot.
44/45/46. November 9 1966 **Albion 5 DOS Utrecht 2** Inter-Cities Fairs Cup (*Brown 3,1 pen, Kaye, Clark*)
13 minutes: Achterberg handled a Hope cross and Brown scores his first Albion penalty.
69 minutes: Brown climbed high to head in a Hope cross.
88 minutes: Drew the keeper to slip the ball past him to complete the only European hat-trick by an Albion player.

47. December 7 1966 **Northampton 1 Albion 3** League Cup (*Simpson, Clark, Brown*)
88 minutes: Came late to slide the ball into the net from a Clark cross.
48. November 26 **Albion 2 Liverpool 1** Division One (*Brown, Clark*)
21 minutes: Brown ran in onto a Clark cross from the left to head into the far corner of the net.
49/50/51. December 26 1966 **Albion 3 Tottenham H 0** (*Brown 3, 1 pen*)
30 minutes: Low cross shot under Jennings' body, from a left wing Kaye cross
49 minutes: Beal fouled Clark in the area, Brown scored his first Albion penalty in the League
60 minutes: The first League hat-trick, a low shot from Astle's cross from the left
52. January 28 1967 **Northampton 1 Albion 3** FA Cup (*Astle, Brown, Clark*)
61 minutes: Clark lays on the perfect pass for Brown to score his first goal in the FA Cup with a rising shot.
53. March 27 1967 **Albion 3 Southampton 2** Division One (*Brown, Clark, Astle*)
20 minutes: A 25 yard snap-shot that bounced in off Martin's chest, the keeper seriously at fault.
54. April 1 1967 **Albion 3 Blackpool 1** Division One (*Brown, Clark, Williams*)
71 minutes: A Kaye through ball beat two defenders for Brown to take in his stride and shoot over Waiters.
55. April 28 1967 **Albion 3 West Ham 1** Division One (*Brown 2, 2 pens, Astle*)
56. May 6 1967 **Blackpool 1 Albion 3** Division One (*Brown pen, Astle, Williams*)
87 minutes: Jones handled a goal bound Kaye shot, Brown scored from the penalty spot.
57/58/59. May 13 1967 **Albion 6 Newcastle United 1** Division One (*Brown 3, Foggo, Williams, Clark*)
38 minutes: Astle prodded the ball through and Brown beat Marshall in a one on one.
44 minutes: Foggo broke away, turning the ball on for Brown to beat Marshall from close range.
69 minutes: A precisely timed header from a left wing Williams cross.

1967-68

August 9 1967 **Bournemouth 0 Albion 1** Pre-season friendly (*Brown*)
60. August 23 1967 **Wolverhampton W 3 Albion 3** Division One (*Brown, Kaye, Foggo*)
90 minutes: Brown punched a high cross from Graham Williams past Phil Parkes into the net
61. September 30 1967 **Albion 4 Sheffield United 1** Division One (*Astle 3, Brown*)
56 minutes: Hodgkinson went down too late to stop Brown's ten yard blast from another Hope pass.
62. October 7 1967 **Fulham 1 Albion 2** Division One (*Brown, Astle*)
70 minutes: Brown ran into a Kaye through ball to score a glorious 20 yard winner at Craven Cottage
63. November 11 1967 **Albion 8 Burnley 1** Division One (*Brown, Hope 2, Clark 2, Brown, Astle, Kaye, Colquhoun*)
24 minutes: Thomson let Brown's first time shot from 20 yards go through his hands and his legs!

The pressure is on; having had his first penalty saved, Tony retakes to score past Stepney in the 6-3 win over Manchester United in 1968

64. December 26 1967 **Albion 3 Manchester City 2** Division One (*Brown, Astle 2*)
37 minutes: Krzywicki headed down a Hope cross for Brown to fire home from ten yards.
65. December 30 **Manchester City 0 Albion 2** Division One (*Brown, Krzywicki*)
87 minutes: Persistence in the tackle won Brown possession to go on to place a shot past Mulhearn.
66. January 6 1968 **Liverpool 4 Albion 1** Division One (*Brown*)
15 minutes: After Hope had hit the bar with a penalty given against Tommy Smith, the referee ordered a retake and Brown placed his low shot wide of the keeper.
67. January 27 1968 **Colchester United 1 Albion 1** FA Cup (*Brown pen*)
38 minutes: A penalty equaliser after Forbes had brought down Astle set Albion *en route* to the Cup Final.
68. February 17 1968 **Albion 1 Southampton 1** FA Cup (*Brown*)
47 minutes: A weak, low shot from 30 yards that Martin stooped to collect, only for the ball to hit a divot and bounce over his shoulder into the net
69. February 21 1968 **Southampton 2 Albion 3** FA Cup (*Astle 2, Brown*)
28 minutes: Gabriel misjudged a Williams cross and Brown volleyed in.
70. February 24: **Albion 2 Fulham 1** Division One (*Brown pen, Astle*)
21 minutes: Clark tripped in the area by Stan Brown, Tony Brown gave Macedo no chance from the spot
71/72: April 15 1968 **Albion 2 Newcastle United 0** Division One (*Brown 2*)
14 minutes: Astle headed down a long Ray Wilson cross and Brown fired in from ten yards
36 minutes: A fortunate goal as Brown's intended cross lopped over Marshall into the net.
73. April 27 1968 **Birmingham 0 Albion 2** FA Cup semi-final at Villa Park (*Astle, Brown*)
67 minutes: Brown beat Herriott with an angled drive from a Hope pass to send Albion to Wembley again
74. April 29 **Albion 6 Manchester United 3** Division One (*Astle 3, Rees, Hartford, Brown pen*)
55 minutes: Stiles downed Rees. Stepney saved the first penalty, but moved and Brown scored at the second attempt
June 1 1968 **Kenya 1 Albion 2** End of Season tour (*Brown 2, 1 pen*)
June 8 1968 **Kenya 3 Albion 4** End of Season tour (*Brown, Hartford, Krzywicki, Collard*)

1968-69

July 30 1968 **Carlisle United 1 Albion 1** Pre-season friendly (*Brown*)
75. August 14 1968 **Albion 3 Manchester United 1** Division One (*Brown, Astle 2*)
8 minutes: Brown out-jumped Astle at the far post to head past Stepney
76. August 17 1968 **Chelsea 3 Albion 1** Division One (*Brown*)
54 minutes: A 25 yard free kick curled around the wall and wide of Peter Bonetti
77. August 27 1968 **Coventry 4 Albion 2** Division One (*Brown, Rees*)
80 minutes: Brown pulled down Lovett's cross to turn and fire home a wonderful goal
78. September 7 1968 **Albion 2 Nottingham Forest 5** Division One (*Brown, Astle*)
86 minutes: Brown volleyed in from fifteen yards after a Rees cross was missed by a defender
79. September 25 1968 **Peterborough United 2 Albion 1** League Cup (*Brown pen*)
82 minutes: Brown beat former team-mate Tony Millington from the spot after Noble downed Clark.
80. October 2 1968 **Albion 2 Bruges 0** ECWC (*Brown, Hartford*)
15 minutes: Astle headed down Hartford's left wing cross for the incoming Brown to shoot home
81. October 9 1968 **Albion 6 Coventry City 1** Division One (*Astle 2, Rees, Brown pen, Hartford, Tudor og*)
48 minutes: Brown sent Glazier the wrong way from the penalty spot after Hill brought down Astle.
82. October 19 1968 **Albion 1 Arsenal 0** Division One (*Brown*)
89 minutes: After Rees had been floored by Storey, Brown fired a brilliant 20 yards free kick just inside the post.
83. November 23 1968 **Manchester City 5 Albion 1** Division One (*Brown*)
68 minutes: Brown won the ball in a challenge with Booth to beat Dowd from ten yards.
84/85. November 27 1968 **Albion 4 Dinamo Bucharest 0** ECWC (*Brown 2, 1 pen, Lovett, Astle*)
44 minutes: Lovett missed a Fraser cross, Brown, following up, put it in via the underside of the bar.
51 minutes: Stoenescu fouled Clark and Brown converted the penalty kick in his usual style.
86. November 30 1968 **Albion 3 Sunderland 0** Division One (*Brown, Rees, Hartford*)
6 minutes: Lovett rounded Montgomery and squared the ball to the waiting Brown for an easy tap-in.
87. December 14 1968 **Albion 1 Leicester City 1** Division One (*Brown pen*)
37 minutes: After Shilton pulled down Kaye, Brown slotted home a well-placed penalty
88. January 18 1969 **Albion 1 Southampton 2** Division One (*Brown pen*)
63 minutes: After Kirkup had flattened Ronnie Rees, Brown dispatched the penalty kick.
89. February 12 **Albion 1 Arsenal 0** FA Cup (*Brown*)
67 minutes: Ian Ure headed a Lovett cross out as far as Brown, who lashed in a left foot volley on the turn

90. March 1 1969 **Chelsea 1 Albion 2** FA Cup (*Brown, Astle*)
28 minutes: Astle headed on a Hope cross for Brown to squeeze in a shot at the far post.
91. March 10 **Sunderland 0 Albion 1** Division One (*Brown*)
41 minutes: Montgomery got in a mess after a big boot down the middle from Talbut, leaving Brown to walk the ball in.
92/93. March 15: **Burnley 2 Albion 2** Division One (*Brown 2*)
23 minutes: Cantello's shot, which was parried by the keeper, was going in anyway, when Brown blasted it into the net a foot off the line.
71 minutes: From a Cantello pass, Brown's shot was saved, but he put in the rebound.
94. April 7 1969 **Albion 4 Tottenham H 3** Division One (*Brown, Astle 2, Hope*)
59 minutes: Astle headed down a Krzywicki cross for Brown to charge in and bundle the ball past Pat Jennings
95. April 14 1969 **Albion 3 West Ham United 1** Division One (*Brown, Astle 2*)
80 minutes: A simple header from a Fraser cross
96. April 19 1969 **Albion 5 Newcastle United 1** (*Kaye, Hartford, Clark, Astle, Brown pen*)
61 minutes: Brown sent McFaul the wrong way from the spot after Burton toppled Clark
97. April 23 1969 **Albion 2 Ipswich Town 2** Division One (*Brown, Astle*)
82 minutes: After Wilson sent Astle away, he squared the ball for Brown to score with a tremendous drive
May 11 1969 **Vancouver All Stars 0 Albion 2** End of season friendly (*Brown 2, 2 pens*)
May 14 1969 **Victoria O'Keefes 1 Albion 4** End of season friendly (*Brown, Kaye, Krzywicki, Hegan*)
May 23 1969 **California Clippers 2 Albion 2** End of season US Tournament (*Brown, Hegan*)

1969-70

98. August 23 1969 **West Ham 1 Albion 3** Division One (*Brown, Suggett, Krzywicki*)
37 minutes: Suggett back-heeled Hughes' long pass and Brown side-stepped Ferguson to score with a low left footer.
99. September 6 **Sunderland 2 Albion 2** Division One (*Brown, Suggett*)
84 minutes: Krzywicki's speed won the ball on the right and Brown turned his cross into the net for the equaliser.
100. October 15 1969 **Albion 4 Bradford City 0** League Cup (*Cantello, Hope, Krzywicki, Brown*)
44 minutes: Calmly headed a perfect Krzywicki pass past Liney in the City goal.
101. October 25 1969 **Albion 2 Manchester United 1** Division One (*Brown, Hope*)
50 minutes: His first shot hit Astle, then bounced back nicely for Brown to lash the ball past Stepney.
102: December 3 1969 **Albion 4 Carlisle United 1** League Cup semi-final (*Hope, Suggett, Brown, Martin*)
67 minutes: Hope touched an indirect free kick to Brown, who scored with a shot from 15 yards.
103: January 3 1970 **Sheffield Wednesday 2 Albion 1** FA Cup (*Brown*)
61 minutes: The goal of a career, a sensational "over the shoulder" half volley from 25 yards from a Martin high ball.
104: January 17 1970 **Liverpool 1 Albion 1** Division One (*Brown*)
66 minutes: Brown drew Lawrence after a Hope pass cut out two defenders, lifted the ball over the keeper to stun the Kop
105: January 28 1970 **Albion 3 Sunderland 1** Division One (*Brown, Astle 2*)
60 minutes: A finely placed header from an inch-perfect Hartford cross
106: March 21: **Burnley 2 Albion 1** Division One (*Brown*)
21 minutes: A Suggett pass beat both Dobson and Angus and Brown scored with a low shot inside the area.
107/108. March 30 1970 **Albion 3 Chelsea 1** Division One (*Brown 2, Astle*)
30 minutes: Brown rammed in the rebound after a Lyndon Hughes shot was blocked.
69 minutes: Brown ran clear on the left to beat Bonetti from an astute Merrick pass.
109/110: April 4 1970 **Albion 4 Nottingham Forest 0** Division One (*Brown 2, Astle, Glover*)
44 minutes: Brown raced past Hindley to blast home a great shot from a Suggett pass.
83 minutes: A superb left footer from a left wing cross from substitute Percy Freeman.
111/112: May 8 1970 **Albion 4 AS Roma 0** Anglo-Italian Tournament (*Brown 2, Hope, Talbut*)
79 minutes: A point blank header from a left wing cross from Bobby Hope
86 minutes: A shot under the Roma keeper, deflected over the line by full-back Bet

1970-71

113/114: August 18 1970 **Nottingham Forest 3 Albion 3** Division One (*Brown 2, Astle*)
15 minutes: A Hope cross was deflected by Chapman for Brown to bundle over the line

As easy as 1-2-3. Tony hits a superb hat-trick against the club he used to support, Manchester United, in a 4-3 win at The Hawthorns in March 1971

87 minutes: Brown volleyed in another Hope cross for a deserved equaliser at the City Ground.
115/116. August 26 1970 **Albion 5 Stoke City 2** Division One (*Brown 2, Astle 2, Reed*)
51 minutes: A 25 yard free kick that swerved past a bemused Gordon Banks
80 minutes: A brilliant Suggett pass that outwitted the entire Stoke defence leaving Brown with an easy chance.
117. September 19 1970 **Arsenal 6 Albion 2** Division One (*Brown, Reed*)
86 minutes: A close range shot for a consolation goal past Bob Wilson
118. September 26 1970 **Albion 2 Derby County 1** Division One (*Brown, McVitie*)
73 minutes: Hope sent Brown away on the left to send an unstoppable shot past Green in the Rams' goal
119. October 3 1970 **Ipswich Town 2 Albion 2** Division One (*Brown, Astle*)
31 minutes: A sharp pass from McVitie, a first time effort from Brown.
120. October 24 1970 **Manchester United 2 Albion 1** Division One (*Brown*)
20 minutes: Astle, put away by Fraser squared the ball for Brown to score off the bar from 12 yards.
121. October 31 1970 **Albion 3 Everton 0** Division One (*Astle, McVitie, Brown*)
72 minutes: An Astle cross from the right, Brown flicked at the ball, which just crossed the line.
122. November 121 1970 **Huddersfield 2 Albion 1** Division One (*Brown*)
9 minutes: Astle headed Hope's cross top McVitie, whose quick pass was fired in by Brown
123. December 5 1970 **Burnley 1 Albion** 1 Division One (*Brown*)
70 minutes: Brown picked up Waldron's back pass to score with a cross-shot from the left edge of the box
124/125/126. December 12 1970 **Albion 3 Tottenham H 1** Division One (*Brown 3, 1 pen*)
48 minutes: Brown slammed in the rebound after Jennings saved from Suggett
77 minutes: Beal fouled Suggett in the area, Brown's penalty beat Jennings for pace
80 minutes: Hartford burst through the middle to hit the post; Astle got the rebound and squared the ball for a devastating right-footer from Brown

127. December 26 1970 **Coventry City 1 Albion 1** Division One (*Brown pen*)
52 minutes: A characteristic penalty in the centre of Glazier's goal
128/129. January 11 1971 **Scunthorpe United 1 Albion 3** FA Cup (*Brown 2, Astle*)
52 minutes: Brown headed a McVitie curler past Barnard at the Old Show Ground
62 minutes: Another McVitie cross controlled by Suggett and laid off for the Bomber to score from 15 yards
130. February 6 1971 **Albion 1 Burnley 0** Division One (*Brown*)
43 minutes: Took a Lovett through ball in his stride and hit the ball past the advancing Tony Waiters.
131/132. February 17 1971 **Tottenham 2 Albion 2** Division One (*Brown 2*)
4 minutes: Brown finished off a breathtaking run by Hartford to register his hundredth League goal.
60 minutes: Brown nipped in between Collins and Beal to tap in a low McVitie cross to start his second hundred
133/134. February 20 1971 **Albion 2 Huddersfield 1** Division One (*Brown 2*)
50 minutes: Brown put away the rebound when a McVitie shot came back off the post
70 minutes: Astle headed down a Hartford free kick and Brown flicked the ball over Lawson.
135. February 27 1971 **Everton 3 Albion 3** Division One (*Brown, Astle, Wile*)
8 minutes: A McVitie shot hit West and was deflected to brown who made no mistake from close range.
136/137/138. March 6 1971 **Albion 4 Manchester United 3** Division One (*Brown 3, Wile*)
32 minutes: Stepney fumbled a Kaye free kick and Brown shot in from 15 yards
46 minutes: Fitzpatrick failed to clear a Hartford shot and Brown slammed in from three yards out
59 minutes: Running onto a long Cumbes clearance, Brown rounded Dunn to crack the ball past Stepney for his only hat-trick against United
139: March 20 1971 **Albion 2 Wolverhampton W 4** Division One (*Brown, McVitie*)
60 minutes: Astle flicked on a Wilson cross for Brown to run between Shaw and McAlle to stroke the ball past Parkes.
140. April 2 1971 **Liverpool 1 Albion 1** Division One (*Brown*)
50 minutes: Ran after an Astle pass down the middle to slip the ball inside Clemence's right hand post.
141. April 17 1971 **Leeds United 1 Albion 2** Division One (*Brown, Astle*)
18 minutes: Controlled a great Suggett pass to fire past Gary Sprake after a Charlton error. The last time that both Brown and Astle were to feature on the scoresheet together.
142. April 24 1971 **Albion 2 Arsenal 2** Division One (*Brown, Hartford*)
86 minutes: Astle set up Brown to score a late leveller from a narrow angle, against the Double winners
April 21 1971 **Albion 4 Athletico Bilbao 2** Testimonial game (*Brown 2, Merrick, Johnson*)
May 4 1971 **Athletico Bilbao 1 Albion 1** Testimonial game (*Brown*)

1971-72

143/144. July 31 1971 **Wrexham 1 Albion 2** Watney Cup (*Brown 2, 1 pen*)
58 minutes: Hartford's centre was flicked on for Brown to score with a close range shot
63 minutes: Tackled from behind by Ingle, Brown got up to fire the penalty to Gaskell's right.
145. August 14 1971 **West Ham United 0 Albion 1** Division One (*Brown*)
38 minutes: Brown ran onto a superb long Hope pass and steered it past Ferguson
146. August 18 1971 **Albion 2 Everton 0** Division One (*Brown, Wile*)
38 minutes: Cumbes' kick was headed on by Astle for Brown to squeeze the ball past Scott, off the post.
147. August 21 1971 **Albion 1 Coventry City 1** Division One (*Brown*)
66 minutes: Astle flicked on another Cumbes kick for Brown to shoot the equaliser just inside the post.
148. August 23 1971 **Manchester United 3 Albion 1** Division One (at Stoke) (*Brown*)
90 minutes: Suggett squared Cantello's pass for Brown to score a consolation goal from close range.
149. September 18 1971 **Albion 1 Ipswich Town 2** Division One (*Brown*)
53 minutes: Wile was impeded in the area. Sivell saved Brown's penalty but Tony followed up to score the rebound off the bar.
150. October 9 1971 **Crystal Palace 0 Albion 2** Division One (*Brown, Gould*)
34 minutes: From a Cantello cross, Brown headed the ball past a motionless Jackson in the Palace goal.
151. November 20 1971 **Tottenham H 3 Albion 2** Division One (*Brown, Gould*)
75 minutes: Daines dropped a Minton cross under pressure from Kaye and Brown put the ball just inside the post.
152. November 27 1971 **Albion 2 Wolverhampton W 3** Division One (*Brown pen, Gould*)
54 minutes: Brown from the spot after a handball offence by Derek Dougan.
153. December 27 1971 **Albion 1 Liverpool 0** Division One (*Brown*)
5 minutes: A Wile lob skidded off the head of Ross for Brown to cleverly lift the ball over Clemence's head.
154. January 1 1972 **Ipswich Town 2 Albion 3** Division One (*Brown, Gould, McVitie*)
61 minutes: Gould chipped over the advancing Best for Brown to tap into the net in a great Albion comeback

155/156. January 8 1972 **Albion 2 Sheffield United 2** Division One (*Brown 2*)
8 minutes: Slid a McVitie low cross into an empty net, with goalkeeper Hope out of position.
72 minutes: 25 yard free kick deflected by defender to send Hope the wrong way.
157. January 15 1972 **Albion 1 Coventry City 2** FA Cup (*Brown*)
59 minutes A McVitie cross from the left hit Brown on the back — he turned quickly to shoot past Glazier
February 2 1972 **Queens Park Rangers 1 Albion 2** Friendly (*Brown, Hartford*)
158. February 12 1972 **Leicester City 0 Albion 1** Division One (*Brown*)
76 minutes: Suggett flicked the ball up high on the edge of the area, Brown brilliantly volleyed high past Shilton
159. February 19 1972 **Albion 3 Southampton 2** Division One (*Brown, Gould, Cantello*)
87 minutes: Vital late winner as Brown ran onto a Wilson through ball to deflect it past Martin.
February 26 1972 **Preston NE 2 Albion 1** Friendly (*Brown*)
160. March 1 1972 **Manchester City 2 Albion 1** Division One (*Brown pen*)
72 minutes: Doyle handled in the area, Brown hammered a typical penalty past Corrigan.
161. April 15 1972 **Wolverhampton W 0 Albion 1** Division One (*Brown*)
1 minute: Tony Brown pounced after an Ally Brown cross shot was pushed out by Parkes
162. April 27 1972 **Albion 4 Chelsea 0** Division One (*T Brown, A Brown, Cantello, Gould*)
27 minutes: Tony Brown ran onto a Gould lob, shrugged off Paddy Mulligan and shot past Bonetti.

1972-73

August 1 1972 **Landskroner Bols 1 Albion 1** Pre-season Tour (*Brown*)
163. September 6 1972 **Albion 2 Queens Park Rangers 1** League Cup (*Brown pen, Evans og*)
27 minutes: Brown beat Parkes from the spot after Gould had had his legs whipped from underneath him
164. September 9 1972 **Albion 2 Derby County 1** Division One (*Brown, Gould*)
67 minutes: After Ally Brown missed a Gould centre, Tony Brown put a cross-shot past Boulton
165. September 30 1973 **Manchester City 2 Albion 1** Division One (*Brown*)
58 minutes: Rodney Marsh made a hash of a back-pass and Brown ran through the middle to beat three defenders and shoot into the corner.
166. October 14 1972 **Chelsea 3 Albion 1** Division One (*Brown, pen*)
59 minutes: Brown beat Bonetti with a penalty given for a foul on Bobby Gould.
167/168. October 25 **Albion 2 Newcastle United 1** Texaco Cup (*Brown 2, 1 pen*)
12 minutes: A penalty after Ian McFaul floored Bobby Gould with a right hook
27 minutes: Ally Brown crossed for his namesake to stoke the ball past McFaul
169. November 11 1972 **Tottenham H 1 Albion 1** Division One (*Brown*)
23 minutes: Challenged Naylor to a Nisbet cross to tuck the loose ball past Daines
170/171. November 25 1972 **Albion 2 Stoke City 1** Division One (*Brown 2, 1 pen*)
28 minutes: Brown beat the advancing Farmer at the near post to a Hartford through ball.
83 minutes: Denis Smith handled a Cantello cross for Brown to score from the spot.
172. December 9 1972 **Albion 1 Liverpool 1** Division One (*Brown*)
69 minutes: Brown ran onto a Wile boot to fire over Clemence, Emlyn Hughes adjudged to have been too late to clear off the line.
173. December 16 1972 **Arsenal 2 Albion 1** Division One (*Brown*)
87 minutes: A consolation goal from a right wing cross from debutant Willie Johnston, Brown's swerver giving Barnett no chance.
174. February 3 1973 **Albion 2 Swindon Town 0** FA Cup (*Brown, Cantello*)
17 minutes: A looping header over young Allen, in goal, from a Johnston cross
175. February 17 1973 **West Ham United 2 Albion 1** Division One (*Brown*)
71 minutes: A poor McDowell clearance fell for Cantello who set up Brown to tap into an empty net.
176. February 28 1973 **Albion 1 Arsenal 0** Division One (*Brown*)
57 minutes: Astle headed down Johnston's cross for Brown to beat Wilson at the post
177. March 10 1973 **Albion 1 Chelsea 1** Division One (*Brown*)
5 minutes: A Cantello mis-hit shot fooled the Chelsea defence to leave Brown with an easy task to beat the stranded Phillips.
178. March 24 1973 **Albion 1 Southampton 1** Division One (*Brown*)
40 minutes: A great dummy from Alan Merrick, letting the ball run through his legs, sent Brown clear to score with a powerful left footer from 20 yards.

1973-74

179/180. August 25 1973 **Blackpool 2 Albion 3** Division Two (*Brown 2, Glover*)
7 minutes: Brown cut in sharply on the right from a Shaw pass to beat George Wood easily.
63 minutes: Another precision pass from Shaw to Brown, who netted with a fierce right footer.
181. September 12 1973 **Sheffield Wednesday 3 Albion 1** Division Two (*Brown*)
19 minutes: Allan Glover fell over in front of goal but still managed to set up Brown for a tap-in.
182. September 15 1973 **Albion 3 Nottingham Forest 3** Division Two (*T Brown, A Brown, Minton*)
69 minutes: Donaghy cross for Glover to volley against the post, Brown tucking away the rebound.
183. October 1 1973 **Preston NE 3 Albion 1** Division Two (*Brown*)
69 minutes: Already three goals down, Brown scored with a good shot on the turn.
184. October 6 1973 **Bristol City 1 Albion 1** Division Two (*Brown*)
25 minutes: Nisbet's throw was back-headed by Shaw for Brown te slip around the keeper to score.
185. October 13 **Albion 1 Carlisle United 1** Division Two (*Brown*)
60 minutes: Hartford's free kick came back off the wall for Brown to score with a rising shot.
186. November 3 1973 **Cardiff City 0 Albion 1** Division Two (*Brown*)
81 minutes: Wile's long headed clearance was picked up by Brown who scored from a narrow angle.
187. November 10 1973 **Albion 2 Notts County 1** Division Two (*Brown, Shaw*)
15 minutes: Brown ran onto a Johnston through ball to score the Albion equaliser.
188/189. December 26 1973 **Albion 2 Aston Villa 0** Division Two (*Brown 2*)
34 minutes: Cumbes saved from Glover, then Brown, who scored at the second attempt.
87 minutes: After a pass from Cantello, Brown's shot squirmed under Cumbes' body.
190/191/192. January 5 1974 **Albion 4 Notts County 0** FA Cup (*Brown 3, Johnston*)
10 minutes: Wile back-headed Glover's corner for Brown to score from point-blank range.
87 minutes: Johnston found Brown running through the middle to drive a low shot past Roy Brown.
90: After teasing the County defence, Brown fired home to complete his only hat-trick in the FA Cup.
193/194/195/196. January 12 1974 **Nottingham Forest 1 Albion 4** Division Two (*Brown 4*)
10 minutes: Hindley's lack of control saw the ball come to Brown who tapped into an unguarded net
36 minutes: A Shaw dummy and Brown took two paces and fired home past Barron.
47 minutes: Hartford's shot was deflected by Shaw to Brown who completed a hat-trick from close-in.
64 minutes: Beating offside, Brown took on Shaw's pass to round Barron for only four goal haul.
197. January 30 1974 **Albion 1 Everton 0** FA Cup (Brown)
38 minutes: A header at the far post from Johnston's corner -- as Shaw impeded the goalkeeper...
198/199. March 2 1974 **Aston Villa 1 Albion 3** Division Two (*Brown 2, 1 pen, Wile*)
25 minutes: Aitkin handled, Brown thumped the penalty into the back of the net.
28 minutes: Ross turned Cantello's cross for Brown to lunge and head a fine goal.
200. March 9 1974 **Bolton Wanderers 1 Albion 1** Division Two (*Brown*)
4 minutes: Astle headed down Wilson's long throw for Brown to score with a fine glancing header.
201. April 27 1974 **Albion 1 Luton Town 1** Division Two (*Brown pen*)
71 minutes: Johnston was flattened by Faulkner, Brown equalised from the penalty spot.
May 6 1974 **Albion/Villa XI 2 Wolves/Blues XI 1** Testimonial (*Brown, Hamilton*)

1974-75

202. August 6 1974 **Albion 5 Norwich City 1** Texaco Cup (*T Brown, A Brown, Shaw, Hughes, Johnston*)

203. September 28 1974 **Albion 3 Oxford United 0** Division Two (*Brown, Merrick, Cantello*)
43 minutes: Brown collected a pass from Mayo and tucked the ball past Wilkins.
204. November 6 1974 **Albion 2 Bristol Rovers 2** Division Two (*Brown, Glover*)
35 minutes: Brown ran onto a Glover pass to put Albion 2-0 ahead.
205. November 30 1974 **Albion 1 Oldham Athletic 0** Division Two (*Brown*)
34 minutes: Mayo headed down Shaw's cross at the far post for Brown to bundle over the line.
206. January 25 1975 **Carlisle United 3 Albion 2** FA Cup (*Brown, pen, Nisbet*)
26 minutes: Johnston was fouled by Train and Brown blasted home the penalty.
207/208. March 8 1975 **Albion 4 Sheffield Wednesday 0** Division Two (*Brown 2, 1 pen, Edwards, Wile*)
47 minutes: Thompson pushed Ian Edwards and Brown scored from the penalty spot.
87 minutes: Edwards returned the compliment to set up Brown to blast home his second.
209. March 15 1975 **Oxford United 1 Albion 1** Division Two (*Brown*)
49 minutes: The neatest of headers at the far post from Glover's left wing cross.

210. March 22 1975 **Albion 2 Portsmouth 1** Division Two (*Brown, Wilson*)
5 minutes: Wilson's long cross met first time by Brown's low volley.
211. March 29 1975 **Aston Villa 3 Albion 1** Division Two (*Brown*)
24 minutes: A rising, curling shot from Brown that Cumbes misjudged and let through.
212/213. April 2 1975 **Albion 4 Notts County 1** Division Two (*Brown 2, 1 pen, Edwards, Cantello*)
61 minutes: Johnston downed by Needham, Brown scored from the spot.
69 minutes: A perfect pass from Cantello, Brown cut inside and scored with an angled shot.
214/215. April 5 1975 **Albion 2 Millwall 1** Division Two (*Brown 2*)
67 minutes: A typical thunderbolt free kick put Albion level.
68 minutes: Johnston weaved his way through and crossed for Brown to slam the winner.

1975-76

216. September 6 1975 **Albion 2 York City 2** Division Two (*Brown, Hurst*)
24 minutes: Johnston picked up a clearance and slid the ball for Brown to score just inside the box.
217. October 25 1975 **Bristol City 0 Albion 2** Division Two (*T Brown, A Brown*)
86 minutes: Out of the blue, way out on the right, Brown rolled the ball wide of Cashley
218. November 15 1975 **Albion 2 Hull City 0** Division Two (*Brown, Martin*)
59 minutes: A glancing header past a groping Wealands from Giles' corner kick
219. December 6 1975 **Albion 3 Portsmouth 1** (*T Brown pen, A Brown 2*)
52 minutes: A Bomber penalty awarded after Cahill had handled a Mulligan shot
220/221. January 3 1976 **Albion 3 Carlisle United 1** FA Cup (*T Brown 2, 1 pen, A Brown*)
82 minutes: Train handles, Burleigh saves Tony's penalty but Brown nets from the rebound
86 minutes: Two goals in four minutes, as Brown broke clear of the defence to score
222. January 24 1976 **Albion 3 Lincoln City 2** FA Cup (*Brown, Martin, Robson*)
2 minutes: Johnston's cross is deflected by Booth to Brown who stabbed home from close range
223. Jan 31 1976 **Chelsea 1 Albion 2** Division Two (*Brown, Martin*)
83 minutes: Ally Brown nods on Johnston's cross for Brown to volley a terrific late winner.
224. February 14 1976 **Albion 1 Southampton 1** FA Cup (*Brown*)
59 minutes: Johnston beta three before pulling back for Brown to score from close range.
225. February 25 1976 **Albion 2 Oxford United 0** Division Two (*Brown, Robertson*)
13 minutes: Picking up a Robson clearance Brown ran 60 yards to score a great goal
226. April 9 1976 **Charlton Athletic 2 Albion 1** Division Two (*Brown pen*)
46 minutes: A Giles header handled by Curtis, Brown's typical penalty equaliser
227. April 24 1976 **Oldham Athletic 0 Albion 1** Division Two (*Brown*)
55 minutes; Martin's cross headed down by Ally for Brown to juggle the ball from left to right to score
April 30 1976 **Walsall 1 Albion 4 Testimonial** (*T. Brown, A. Brown, Edwards 2*)
May 4 1976 **Albion 5 Coventry City 1** Friendly (*T. Brown 2, A Brown, Johnston, Rushbury*)

1976-77

August 2 1976 **Crewe Alexandra 2 Albion 6** Friendly (*T Brown pen, A Brown 2, Cantello, Mayo, Nisbet*)
228. August 21 1976 **Leeds United 2 Albion 2** Division One (*T Brown, A Brown*)
43 minutes: Mayo headed on a Giles cross for Brown to score from close range
229. August 28 1976 **Albion 2 Norwich City 0** Division One (*T Brown pen, A Brown*)
47 minutes: Brown was bundled over by Steele, chasing a Giles pass; he beat Keelan from the spot
230. September 11 1976 **Birmingham City 0 Albion 1** Division One (*Brown*)
60 minutes: A superb, out of the blue shot from nearly thirty yards
231. October 2 1976 **Albion 4 Tottenham H 2** Division One (*Brown pen, Treacy, Martin 2*)
53 minutes: Steads handled Johnston's cross, Brown slammed the penalty past Jennings
232. November 27 1976 **Albion 3 Everton 0** Division One (*Brown, Cross, Treacy*)
5 minutes: Brown accelerated onto a first time pass from Treacy to score from the edge of the box
233. January 22 1977 **Albion 1 Leeds United 2** Division One (*Brown pen*)
59 minutes: Hampton tripped Cantello in the area and Brown smashed home the penalty
234. May 7 1977 **Leicester City 0 Albion 5** Division One (*Brown, Cunningham, Cross, Martin 2*)
81 minutes: Brown lunged to head in after Ally Brown's shot had been blocked
235. May 16 1977 **Everton 1 Albion 1** Division One (*Brown*)
60 minutes: Brown ran on to sweep a superb Mick Martin through ball past Dai Davies

1977-78

236/237. August 6 1977 **St Mirren 3 Albion 4** Tennant-Caledonian Cup (*Brown 2, 1 pen, Cross, Robson*)
12 minutes: Robson was tripped by Richardson and Brown gave Hunter no chance from the spot
50 minutes: Cunningham headed a Robson cross against the bar and Brown snapped up the rebound
238/239. August 20 1977 **Albion 3 Chelsea 0** Division One (*Brown 2, 1 pen, Cross*)
63 minutes: Cross was pushed by Wicks and Brown opened the scoring from the spot
79 minutes: Johnston played forward to Brown who scored with an unstoppable shot on the run
240. September 17 1977 **Albion 2 Wolverhampton W 2** Division One (*Brown pen, Cross*)
15 minutes: Cross was brought down by Parkes, Brown sent his old adversary the wrong way
241/242. September 24 1977 **Albion 3 Birmingham City 1** Division One (*Brown 2, 1 pen, Regis*)
2 minutes: A rising shot after Regis had nodded down Johnston's centre
76 minutes: Montgomery brought down Brown, who stepped up to fire home the penalty
243/244. October 1 1977 **Coventry City 1 Albion 2** Division One (*Brown 2*)
66 minutes: Tony shot after Ally Brown had hit the bar, the ball going in off Jim Holton
84 minutes: This time Johnston hit the bar and Brown beat Oakey in the race to head the rebound in
245. October 4 1977 **Everton 3 Albion 1** Division One (*Brown pen*)
44 minutes: An innocuous offence gave Tony Brown a penalty with which he beat George Wood
246. October 25 1977 **Albion 1 Watford 0** League Cup (*Brown*)
52 minutes: A matchwinner, rifled in on the run from 20 yards to save struggling Albion
247. November 5 1977 **Albion 2 Leicester City 0** Division One (*Brown, Cross*)
14 minutes: A right foot volley after a succession of five corners
December 13 1977 **Saudi Arabia 0 Albion 1** Friendly (*Brown*)
248. December 26 1977 **Bristol City 3 Albion 1** Division One (*Brown*)
3 minutes: Brown robbed Norman Hunter to fire home from twelve yards
249. December 31 1977 **Albion 1 Leeds United 0** Division One (*Brown pen*)
85 minutes: Martin was pushed in the back in the area and Brown made no mistake with the penalty
250. January 2 1978 **Chelsea 2 Albion 2** Division One (*T Brown, A Brown*)
90 minutes: Mick Martin crossed for Tony Brown to "toe-end" a late, late equaliser
251. January 7 1978 **Albion 4 Blackpool 1** FA Cup (*Brown pen, Johnston 2, Regis*)
69 minutes: Brown sent Ward the wrong way from the spot after Regis had been brought down
252. February 1 1978 **Albion 3 Manchester United 2** FA Cup (*Brown, Regis 2*)
14 minutes: Tony Brown swept the ball home after Ally Brown headed down Johnston's cross
253. February 28 1978 **Birmingham City 1 Albion 2** Division One (*T Brown, A Brown*)
33 minutes: Ally Brown headed on Godden's kick and Tony Brown swept home his 200th League goal
254/255. March 4 1978 **Ipswich Town 2 Albion 2** Division One (*T Brown 2, 1 pen*)
55 minutes: Osman took Regis' legs and Brown beat Cooper from the spot
89 minutes: Ally Brown squared a Johnston long ball for Brown to turn it home from close range
256. March 27 1978 **Albion 2 Bristol City 1** Division One (*Brown, Johnston*)
90 minutes: A three man build up ended with a fine left foot shot from 15 yards
257. April 1 1978 **Leicester City 0 Albion 1** Division One (*Brown*)
71 minutes: Brown, looking well offside, took a Regis pass to round Wallington and tap into an empty net
258. April 8 1978 **Ipswich Town 3 Albion 1** FA Cup semi-final (*Brown pen*)
76 minutes; Hunter handled Martin's cross for Brown to pull a goal back from the spot
259. April 18 1978 **Albion 1 Derby County 0** Division One (*Brown pen*)
74 minutes; Gerry Ryan fouled Brown in the area, the Bomber sent Middleton the wrong way
260. May 2 1978 **Albion 2 Nottingham Forest 2** Division One (*Brown, Hughes*)
28 minutes: Brown's 25 yard shot skidded off the wet turf to beat Peter Shilton
May 26 1978 **Kwantung Province 0 Albion 6** Chinese Tour (*Brown, Regis 2, Wile, Martin, Cunningham*)
May 28 1978 **Hong Kong 0 Albion 3** Chinese Tour (*Brown, Regis, Chi-Keung og*)

1978-79

August 3 1978 **Motherwell 1 Albion 8** Testimonial (*T Brown, Cunningham 3, A Brown 3, Stevens og*)
August 13 1978 **Damascus Police 1 Albion 1** Pre-season Tour (*Brown*)
261. August 19 1978 **Albion 2 Ipswich Town 1** Division One (*T Brown, A Brown*)
62 minutes: Brown put the finishing touch to a ball that was already going in off George Burley
262. September 30 1978 **Chelsea 1 Albion 3** Division One (*Brown, Regis, Wile*)
59 minutes: A left footer from Robson's chip, to equal the Ronnie Allen League goals record

Tony scores his last League goals for the Albion, in the 4-1 home win over Coventry on October 27 1979. Left, beating Jim Holton to score, and right, beating Les Sealey from the spot.

263. October 14 1978 **Leeds United 1 Albion 3** Division One (*Brown, Regis 2*)
39 minutes: A shot from 25 yards, via the post, beating Harvey for Tony's 209th League goal
264. October 21 1978 **Albion 7 Coventry City 1** Division One (*Brown, Cunningham 2, Regis 2, Statham, Cantello*)
75 minutes: A tremendous right footer from a neat sideways pass from Robson
265. November 25 1978 **Albion 1 Aston Villa 1** Division One (*Brown pen*)
37 minutes: The overlapping Batson was brought down by Craig, Brown made no mistake from the spot
266/267. December 6 1978 **Albion 2 Valencia 0** UEFA Cup (*Brown 2, 1 pen*)
4 minutes: Handball by Cordero, a classic penalty by Brown
80 minutes: Cunningham brilliantly cut the ball back for Brown to volley in first time
268. December 16 1978 **Wolverhampton W 0 Albion 3** Division One (*T Brown, A Brown 2*)
57 minutes: Cantello's cross found Brown who picked his spot from 25 yards
269/270. December 30 1978 **Manchester United 3 Albion 5** Division One (*Brown 2, Regis, Cunningham, Cantello*)
26 minutes: Ally Brown's dummied deceived for Tony Brown to sweep the ball past Bailey
45 minutes: Cantello headed on Statham's cross and Brown nudged the ball over the line
271/272. January 15 1979 **Albion 4 Coventry City 0** FA Cup (*T Brown 2, Batson, A Brown*)
17 minutes: Statham and Regis both had shots blocked; Brown made no mistake with the rebound
80 minutes: Slotted home coolly from Bryan Robson's through ball
273. February 24 1979 **Albion 1 Leeds United 2** Division One (*Brown*)
37 minutes: Cantello back-heeled Wile's header on for Brown to score a great first time volley
274. April 14 1979 **Albion 1 Arsenal 1** Division One (*Brown*)
57 minutes: Regis headed Cunningham's cross down and Brown back-headed into the net
May 29 1979 **Fyn Boldspil XI 1 Albion 4** Close season tour (*Brown 2, Regis 2*)
May 31 1979 **IHF 0 Albion** 7 Close season tour (*T Brown, A Brown 2, Cunningham 2, Regis 2*)

1979-80

275. September 26 **Albion 2 Coventry City 1** League Cup (*T Brown pen, Wile*)
22 minutes: Robson was brought down by Sealey, Brown beat the keeper easily from the spot
276/277. October 27 1979 **Albion 4 Coventry City 1** Division One (*T Brown 2, 1 pen, A Brown*)
86 minutes: A classic Bomber penalty, sending Les Sealey the wrong way from the spot
89 minutes: Brown slid home his final Albion League goal from an Ally Brown cross
278. January 8 1980 **West Ham United 2 Albion 1** FA Cup (*Brown*)
86 minutes: A header from a cross by Peter Barnes — Tony's last first class Albion goal

1980-81

279. June 21 1980 **New England Tea Men 3 Minnesota 2** (*Brown, Turner, Moen*)

280. June 23 1980 **New England Tea Men 2 Rochester 0** (*Brown, Moen*)
281. June 28 1980 **New England Tea Men 4 Philadelphia 0** (*Brown, Newton 3*)
282. July 1 1980 **Houston 1 New England Tea Men 2** (*Brown, Moen*)
283. July 5 1980 **New England Tea Men 3 San Jose 1** (*Brown, Weller, Newton*)
284. July 16 1980 **Rochester 0 New England Tea Men 1** (*Brown*)
285. August 2 1980 **New England Tea Men 2 Portland 1** (*Brown, Newton*)
286. August 13 1980 **California 1 New England Tea Men 4** (*Brown, Cantillo, Newton 2*)
December 8 1980 **Barnet 0 Albion 5** Testimonial (*Brown, Mills, Trewick, Regis, Deehan*)
287. May 8 1981 **Fort Lauderdale 2 Jacksonville Tea Men 1** (*Brown*)
288. May 9 1981 **Jacksonville Tea Men 1 Atlanta 2** (*Brown*)
289. May 23 1981 **Jacksonville Tea Men 2 Tampa 0** (*Brown, Berrio*)
290. June 6 1981 **Tulsa 2 Jacksonville Tea Men 3** (*Brown, Zec 2*)
291/292. June 9 1981 **Jacksonville Tea Men 4 California 0** (*Brown 2, Green 2*)
293. July 7 1981 **Jacksonville Tea Men 2 Seattle 1** (*Brown, Green*)
294. July 11 1981 **Jacksonville Tea Men 4 San Jose 3** (*Brown, Green 2, Marasco*)
295. August 19 1981 **Edmonton 0 Jacksonville Tea Men 5** (*Brown, Berrio, Zec, Green 2*)

1981-82

296. November 3 1981 **Halifax 1 Torquay 2** Division Four (*Brown, Bourne*)
297. December 5 1981 **Torquay 1 Bury 1** Division Four (*Brown*)
298. January 3 1982 **Aldershot 1 Torquay 1** Division Four (*Brown*)
299. March 6 1982 **Tranmere Rovers 1 Torquay 1** Division Four (*Brown*)
300. April 3 1982 **Sheffield United 4 Torquay 1** Division Four (*Brown*)
301. April 10 1982 **Torquay 1 Peterborough U 2** Division Four (*Brown*)
302. April 17 1982 **Bury 0 Torquay 1** Division Four (*Brown*)
303. April 24 1982 **Torquay 1 Stockport 0** Division Four (*Brown*)
304. April 27 1982 **Torquay 2 Halifax Town 2** Division Four (*Brown, Jones*)
305. May 5 1982 **Torquay 1 Darlington 2** Division Four (*Brown*)
306. May 8 1982 **Torquay 2 Aldershot 1** Division Four (*Brown, Tainton*)

It's there — Tony, bottom right, turns to celebrate what turned out to be his last goal in an Albion shirt, in the FA Cup against West Ham at Upton Park in 1980

TONY BROWN'S APPEARANCES IN ALL COMPETITIONS FOR WEST BROMWICH ALBION

	LEAGUE	FAC	FLC	ICFC	ECWC	UEFA	CS	AIT	Tex	Wat	ASC	TennCal	Others	**TOTAL**
1963-4	13(5)	-	-	-	-	-	-	-	-	-	-	-	-	13(5)
1964-5	17(9)	-	-	-	-	-	-	-	-	-	-	-	3+1(2)	20+1(11)
1965-6	35(17)	1	9(10)	-	-	-	-	-	-	-	-	-	8+1(3)	53+1(30)
1966-7	31(14)	2(1)	4(1)	3(3)	-	-	-	-	-	-	-	-	1	41(19)
1967-8	35(11)	10(4)	1	-	-	-	-	-	-	-	-	-	9(4)	55(19)
1968-9	42(17	4(2)	2(1)	-	6(3)	-	1	-	-	-	-	-	7(5)	62(28)
1969-0	40(10	1(1)	8+1(2)	-	-	-	-	4(2)	-	-	-	-	4	57+1(15)
1970-1	42(28	4(2)	2	-	-	-	-	4	2	-	-	-	4(3)	58(33)
1971-2	40(17	1(1)	1	-	-	-	-	-	-	3(2)	-	-	3(2)	48(22)
1972-3	38+1(12)	5(1)	3(1)	-	-	-	-	-	4(2)	-	-	-	6(1)	56+1(17)
1973-4	41(19	4(4)	2	-	-	-	-	-	-	-	-	-	4(1)	51(24)
1974-5	32+2(12)	3(1)	2	-	-	-	-	-	3(1)	-	-	-	2	42+2(14)
1975-6	37+3(8)	4(4)	1	-	-	-	-	-	-	-	1	-	5+1(3)	48+4(15)
1976-7	36+1(8)	2	3	-	-	-	-	-	-	-	3	-	5(1)	49+1(9)
1977-8	41(19)	6(3)	2(1)	-	-	-	-	-	-	-	-	1(2)	8+1(3)	58+1(28)
1978-9	29+2(10)	6(2)	1	-	-	5+1(2)	-	-	-	-	-	2	12(5)	55+3(19)
1979-0	12+4 2)	+1(1)	5(1)	-	-	2	-	-	-	-	-	-	8+1	22+7(5)
1980-1	-	-	-	-	-	-	-	-	-	-	-	-	3+2(1)	3+2(1)
TOTAL	561+13(218)	53+1(27)	46+1(27)	3(3)	6(3)	7+1(2)	1	8(2)	9(3)	3(2)	4	3(2)	92+7(34)	**803+23(313)**

Abbreviations: FLC: League Cup, ICFC: Inter-Cities Fairs Cup, CS: FA Charity Shield, AIT: Anglo-Italian Tournament, Tex: Texaco Cup, Wat: Watney Cup, ASC: Anglo-Scottish Cup, TennCal: Tennant-Caledonian Cup FLT: Football League Trophy

TONY BROWN'S APPEARANCES AND GOALS FOR THE ALBION RESERVES

	APPEARANCES	GOALS
1962-3	1	1
1963-4	18	13
1964-5	20	22
1965-6	3	5
1966-7	1	1
1967-8	2	-
1975-6	2	5
1976-7	1	-
1979-0	4	2
1980-1	13	2
1981-2	1	1
TOTAL	66	51

TONY BROWN'S APPEARANCES AND GOALS FOR THE TEA MEN

	Apps	Goals	Assists	Points
1981	28+4	8	14	30
1982	36+1	9	10	28
TOTAL	64+5	17	24	58

TONY BROWN'S APPEARANCES AND GOALS FOR TORQUAY

	League	LC	FAC	FLT	Fr
1981-82	34(11)	0	2	2	1
1982-83	4+7	1	0	0	0
TOTAL	38+7(11)	1	2	2	1

TONY BROWN'S APPEARANCES AND GOALS FOR STAFFORD

	Alliance	Friendlies
1982-83	10(3)	1
TOTAL	10(3)	1

TONY BROWN'S PENALTIES FOR THE ALBION

1	Nov 9 1966	H DOS Utrecht ICFC	Hans Hoogeveen
2	Dec 26 1966	H Tottenham	Pat Jennings
3	Mar 27 1967	H Southampton	Eric Martin **missed**
4	April 28 1967	H West Ham	Jim Standen
5	April 28 1967	H West Ham	Jim Standen
6	May 6 1967	A Blackpool	Kevin Thomas
7	Aug 23 1967	A Wolves	Phil Parkes **saved**
8	Jan 6 1968	A Liverpool	Tommy Lawrence
9	Jan 27 1968	A Colchester FAC	Ernie Adams
10	Feb 24 1968	H Fulham	Tony Macedo
11	Apr 29 1968	H Man Utd	Alex Stepney
12	June 1 1968	A Kenya Fr	Not known
13	June 1 1968	A Kenya Fr	Not known
14	Sep 25 1968	A Peterborough LC	Tony Millington
15	Oct 9 1968	H Coventry	Bill Glazier
16	Nov 27 1968	H D Bucharest ECWC	Ille Datcu
17	Dec 14 1968	H Leicester	Peter Shilton
18	Jan 18 1969	H Southampton	Gerry Gurr
19	Mar 1 1969	A Chelsea FAC	Peter Bonetti **saved**
20	April 19 1969	H Newcastle	Iam McFaul
21	May 11 1969	A Vancouver Fr	Barry Sadler
22	May 111969	A Vancouver Fr	Peter Bonetti
23	Oct 29 1969	H Man U	Alex Stepney **saved**
24	Dec 12 1970	H Tottenham	Pat Jennings
25	Dec 26 1970	A Coventry	Bill Glazier
26	July 31 1971	A Wrexham WC	Dave Gaskell
27	Sep 18 1971	H Ipswich	Laurie Sivell **saved, scored rebound**
28	Nov 27 1971	H Wolves	Phil Parkes
29	March 1 1972	A Man City	Joe Corrigan
30	Sep 6 1972	H QPR LC	Phil Parkes
31	Oct 7 1972	H Man Utd	Alex Stepney **missed**
32	Oct 14 1972	A Chelsea	Peter Bonetti
33	Oct 25 1972	H Newcastle Texaco	Iam McFaul
34	Nov 25 1972	H Stoke	John Farmer
35	April 7 1973	H Leicester	Peter Shilton **saved**
36	Mar 2 1974	A Aston Villa	Jim Cumbes
37	April 27 1974	H Luton Town	Graham Horn
38	Jan 25 1975	A Carlisle FAC	Alan Ross
39	March 8 1975	H Sheff Wed	Peter Fox
40	April 2 1975	H Notts Co	Eric McManus
41	Jan 3 1976	H Carlisle FAC	Martin Burleigh **saved, scored rebound**
42	April 9 1976	A Charlton	Jeff Wood
43	Aug 2 1976	A Crewe Fr	Geoff Crudgington
44	Aug 28 1976	H Norwich	Kevin Keelan
45	Oct 2 1976	H Tottenham	Pat Jennings
46	Jan 22 1977	H Leeds Utd	David Harvey
47	Aug 6 1977	A St Mirren TC	David Hunter
48	Aug 20 1977	H Chelsea	David Phillips
49	Sep 17 1977	H Wolves	Phil Parkes
50	Sep 24 1977	H Birmingham	Jim Montgomery
51	Oct 4 1977	A Everton	George Wood
52	Nov 5 1977	H Leicester	Mark Wallington **missed**
53	Dec 31 1977	H Leeds Utd	Dave Stewart
54	Jan 7 1978	H Blackpool FAC	Bob Ward
55	Mar 4 1978	A Ipswich	Paul Cooper
56	April 8 1978	A Ipswich FAC	Paul Cooper
57	April 18 1978	H Derby Co	John Middleton
58	April 25 1978	H Everton	George Wood **missed**
59	Nov 25 1978	H Villa	Jimmy Rimmer
60	Dec 6 1978	H Valencia UEFA	Fernandez Manzanedo
61	Oct 27 1979	H Coventry	Les Sealey

Tony scored 51 penalties out of 61 that he took for the Albion in all matches. Four were missed, and four were saved, by Alex Stepney, Phil Parkes, Peter Shilton and Peter Bonetti. Another two were saved, by Martin Burleigh and Laurie Sivell, only for Tony to net the rebound. Tony also took part in two penalty shoot-outs for the Albion, against Colchester on August 7 1971 (Watney Cup Final) and Southampton (Tennant Caledonina Cup semi-final) on August 5 1978. Tony, of course, scored both times, against Graham Smith and Peter Wells, but Albion lost both shoot-outs, 3-4 and 1-3 respectively.

The Goalkeeper's Fear of the Penalty
Top, Tony blasts a great spot-kick past Coventry's Bill Glazier on Boxing Day 1971.
Left: a rare miss, as Tony skies over the bar with Everton's George Wood on the deck, April 1978.
Bottom: Tony took part in two penalty shoot-outs with the Albion. On both occasions, against Colchester and Southampton, he was successful, which is more than could be said for his team mates, who missed five of their seven attempts. Here Tony hits the spot against Southampton at Ibrox Park, in the Tennant Caledonian Cup semi-final, in August 1978.

TONY BROWN'S REPRESENTATIVE GAMES

Football League 5 Irish League 0

(Norwich, September 23 1970, 20,743)

Football league: Shilton (Leicester), Edwards (Man Utd) [Sub: Smith (Stoke)], Robson (Derby), Nish (Leicester), Sadler (Man Utd), Harvey (Everton), Coates (Burnley), Hector (Derby), Astle (Albion), Peters (Tottenham), Moore (Forest)[Sub: Tony Brown (Albion)]

Irish League: Nicholson (Crusaders), Patton (Glenavon), McKeag (Glentoran), Stewart (Ballymena), McCullogh (Glentoran), O'Doherty (Coleraine), Humphries (Ards), Mullen (Coleraine), Millen (Linfield), Jamison (Crusaders), Cathcart (Linfield). **Scorers: Peters, Astle 2, Brown, Hector.**

Scottish League 0 Football League 1

(Hampden Park, Glasgow, March 17 1971, 17,657)

Football League: Jackson (Crystal Palace), Reaney (Leeds), Parkin (Wolves), Hollins (Chelsea), McFarland (Derby), Moore (West Ham), Coates (Burnley), Brown (Albion), Hurst (West Ham), O'Neill (Southampton), Moore (Forest)

Scottish League: Clark (Aberdeen), Dixon (Kilmarnock), Hay (Celtic), Forsyth (Motherwell)[Sub: Connelly (Celtic)], McKinnon (Rangers), Brogan (Celtic), McLean (Kilmarnock), Callaghan (Celtic), Robb (Aberdeen), Jarvie (Airdrie), Ford (Hearts). **Scorer: Coates**

England 0 Wales 0

(Wembley May 19 1971, 85,000)

England: Shilton (Leicester), Lawler (Liverpool), Cooper (Leeds), Smith, Lloyd, Hughes (all Liverpool), Lee (Man City), Brown (Albion) [Sub: Clarke (Leeds) 74 mins], Hurst (West ham), Coates (Tottenham), Peters (Tottenham)

Wales: Sprake (Leeds), Rodrigues (Sheff Wed), Thomas (Swindon), James (Blackpool), Roberts (Arsenal), Yorath (Leeds), Phillips (Cardiff), Durban (Derby), Davies (Southampton), Toshack (Liverpool), Reece (Sheff Utd) [Sub: Rees (Coventry) 85 mins]

TONY BROWN'S RECORDS

ALBION LEAGUE APPEARANCES

1.	**Tony Brown**	**561+13**
2.	Ally Robertson	504+2
3.	John Wile	499+1
4.	Jesse Pennington	455
5.	Tommy Glidden	445
6.	Len Millard	436
7.	Joe Smith	434
8.	Ronnie Allen	415
9.	Joe Carter	114
10.	Ray Barlow	403

ALBION FA CUP APPEARANCES

1.	**Tony Brown**	**53+1**
2.	Ray Barlow	47
3.	Ronnie Allen	43
4.	Len Millard	41
5.	Billy Bassett	40
6.	Jem Bayliss	39
7.	Jesse Pennington	39
8.	Charlie Perry	39
9.	Joe Reader	39
10.	Joe Carter	37

ALBION EUROPEAN APPEARANCES

1.	**Tony Brown**	**16+1**
2.	Brendan Batson	12
3.	Tony Godden	12
4.	Ally Robertson	12
5.	Bryan Robson	12
6.	Derek Statham	12
7.	John Wile	12
8.	Jeff Astle	10
9.	Ally Brown	10
10.	Cyrille Regis	10

ALBION LEAGUE CUP APPEARANCES

1.	Ally Robertson	53
2.	**Tony Brown**	**46+1**
3.	John WIle	42
4.	Derek Statham	34
5.	John Kaye	31
6.	Doug Fraser	29
7.	Bobby Hope	29
8.	Jeff Astle	28
9.	Ally Brown	27
10.	Tony Godden	27

Tony played in a record 459 First Division games for the Albion, 44 ahead of Ronnie Allen and also holds the record for the most appearances by any player at The Hawthorns (282 games), making his last appearance there against Coventry in December 1979. Only two other players in Albion's history have reached the 500 League game mark — John Wile (500) and Ally Robertson (506)

ALBION LEAGUE SCORERS

1. Tony Brown	**218**
2. Ronnie Allen	208
3. WG Richardson	202
4. Derek Kevan	157
5. Joe Carter	145
6. Jeff Astle	137
7. Tommy Glidden	135
8. Freddie Morris	112
9. Jimmy Cookson	103
10. Dave Walsh	94

ALBION FA CUP SCORERS

1.	**Tony Brown**	**27**
2.	W G Richardson	26
3.	Jem Bayliss	24
4.	Ronnie Allen	23
5.	Derek Kevan	16
6.	Jeff Astle	14
7.	Tom Pearson	12
8.	Joe Wilson	12
9.	Billy Bassett	11
10.	Joe Carter	10

MOST LEAGUE APPEARANCES AT THE HAWTHORNS

1.	**Tony Brown**	**283**
2.	Ally Robertson	256
3.	John Wile	248
4.	Jesse Pennington	230
5.	Tomy Glidden	221
6.	Joe Smith	220
7.	Len Millard	217
8.	Joe Carter	210
9.	Ronnie Allen	205
10.	Ray Barlow	203

MOST APPEARANCES IN ALL COMPETITIONS

1.	**Tony Brown**	**711+16**
2.	Len Millard	627
3.	Ally Robertson	622+4
4.	John Wile	618+1
5.	Jesse Pennington	496
6.	Ray Barlow	482
7.	Tommy Glidden	479
8.	Joe Smith	471
9.	Ronnie Allen	458
10.	Joe Carter	451

MOST LEAGUE GOALS AT THE HAWTHORNS

1.	**Tony Brown**	**128**
2.	W G Richardson	122
3.	Ronnie Allen	110
4.	Joe Carter	95
	Derek Kevan	95
6.	Jeff Astle	90
	Tommy Glidden	90
8.	Fred Morris	72
9.	Dave Walsh	59
10.	Jimmy Cookson	57

ALBION EUROPEAN SCORERS

1.	**Tony Brown**	**8**
2.	Laurie Cunningham	4
3.	Asa Hartford	3
4.	Cyrille Regis	3
5.	Bryan Robson	2

ALBION LEAGUE CUP SCORERS

1.	Jeff Astle	19
2.	**Tony Brown**	**17**
3.	Cyrille Regis	16
4.	Clive Clark	10
5.	Bobby Hope	7